M000073576

FOREVER

Stories of
Real People
Finding Jesus

JAMES STUART BELL
Author of *A Cup of Comfort Devotional*
and Jeanette Gardner Littleton

Adams Media
Avon, Massachusetts

Copyright ©2006, F+W Publications, Inc.
All rights reserved. This book, or parts thereof, may not be reproduced in
any form without permission from the publisher; exceptions are made for
brief excerpts used in published reviews.

Published by
Adams Media, an F+W Publications Company
57 Littlefield Street, Avon, MA 02322. U.S.A.
www.adamsmedia.com

ISBN 10: 1-59869-050-7
ISBN 13: 978-1-59869-050-7

Printed in the United States of America.

J I H G F E D C B A

Library of Congress Cataloging-in-Publication Data
is available from the publisher.

All Scripture quotations in this volume are
from the King James Version of the Bible.

*This book is available at quantity discounts for bulk purchases.
For information, please call 1-800-289-0963.*

SPECIAL THANKS TO Michal Needham, for her invaluable contribution in the areas of compiling and editing.

TO MY SISTER Cathy, who tells stranger and friend alike about the good news found in Jesus Christ.

~ *James Stuart Bell*

DEDICATED TO THE memory of my mom, Ila Elnora Gardner, who lived her faith quietly but steadily until she went to see Jesus face to face; and to my dad, Thurman Gardner, who just met Jesus last Christmas, a month before he died. . . . And to my husband Mark, who introduced my father to the heavenly father.

~ *Jeanette Gardner Littleton*

Contents

Introduction ix

Like Son, Like Father 1
Frank Coppaletta, as told to Pam Meyers

Dirty Laundry 6
Cynthia L. D'Agostino

Fighting the Good Fight 12
Somchai Soonthornturasuk, as told to Rita Stella Galieh

Born Again? Oh No!. 17
Gay Sorensen

A Worthwhile Life. 21
Rev. Thomas C. Lacy

The School Board Meeting That Changed My Life 26
Joyce Starr Macias

The Collision 31
Albert Haley

Freedom Found 37
Barbara Curtis

Those Who Believe 43
Clement Hanson

Daddy's Girl 49
Evelyn Rhodes Smith

Back from the Wild Side 55
Rick Stock, as told to Jeanette Gardner Littleton

Seeking Security 60
Mary A. Hake

What My Students Taught Me 64
Debbie Bentley

How I Found True Love 68
Susan A. J. Lyttek

Return to My Father 73
Ted Hake, as told to Mary A. Hake

He Knew Me 77
Shana L. Merriss

Convicted at a Concert 83
Jo Franz

The God Who Knocks with Kindness 88
Melissa Fields

A Night up in Smoke 92
Mark Littleton

Forever Safe 96
Jan Potter

On the Trail to Truth 99
Suha Gibson, as told to Evangeline Beals Gardner

No Longer Adrift. 104
Lynn Ludwick

Change of Heart. 109
Kurt A. Miesner

Drawn by Love 114
Kelli Pratt, as told to Ronica Stromberg

The Voice of the Future. 119
B. J. Leffall-McGibboney

Clean at Last: Inside and Out 124
Ed Stevenson, as told to Susan J. Reinhardt

God and the Marriage Mess 128
Elizabeth Montes

Finding My Own Faith 135
Reneé W. Hixson

Finding Christ at the Carnival 139
Sonja Herbert

Missing Person—Found by God 147
Michelle Steele, as told to Ronica Stromberg

The Silent Sentinel 151
David R. Simerson

Learning to Give Up 156
Ardy Kolb

Faith in My Sleeve 162
Prem Chand Daniel, as told to Karen Strand

The F.A.T. Girl in the Mirror 168
Kimberly Davidson

The Measure of a Man............................... 175
Harold E. Morgan

When Excelling Isn't Enough........................ 180
Caroline Seunghee Roberts

From the Good Life to a Better Life 186
Michele Starkey

Set Free 189
Gary Carlson, as told to Becky Lyles

Hopeless to Hopeful 196
Diana Lee

Belonging to the Lord 200
Mara Kim

A Whisper in the Silence 205
Candy Arrington

The High That Lasts 209
Batt Stout, as told to Sue Foster

Never Good Enough................................ 212
Judy Burford

Looking for My Father 215
Alma Barkman

Righteousness for the Right Reasons................... 220
Willie Kanthenga

God's Reality Show 224
Jeanette M. Bakke

New Life... 230
Marion E. Gorman

Safely in His Hands 233
Elsi Dodge

An Instrument God Uses 238
George Elias Galieh

Pilgrimage Home.................................. 244
Anita Estes

Losing Control to Find It 249
Lynn M. Stout

When God Enters the Stepfamily..................... 255
Maxine Marsolini

A Different Destiny................................ 261
Cheryl Gochnauer

Introduction

"It's NOT SUPPOSED to be this way," my eighty-six-year-old dad moaned to my husband, Mark. For months Dad had been in either a skilled nursing facility or the hospital with heart attacks, pneumonia, and infections. But few procedures seemed to help. Dad's body was wearing out.

"Well, Pops," Mark replied, using his affectionate nickname for dad. "Your body is getting tired. This happens when people start to enter their last days."

"I've been thinking about Jesus," Dad croaked. Dad had always respected God, but kept him at a distance. Mark had encouraged him months earlier to think about entering a relationship with Jesus. At that stage of his life, Dad couldn't talk very easily. But that December day in 2005, Dad told Mark he wanted to know Jesus.

"Do you want me to pray for you, Pops? Do you want me to help you ask Jesus into your heart?"

Dad nodded. Mark prayed, telling God that Dad wanted to know Jesus as his savior and friend.

"I do!" Dad suddenly burst out, sounding just like a groom at the altar.

"It is kind of like getting married, Pops, isn't it?" Mark said. "You're entering a relationship that will last forever."

We noticed a subtle change in Dad's life after that day, and he celebrated his first Christmas knowing the one who Christmas is all about.

The day after Christmas, Dad was in the ER again. His pain was relentless as we listened to a child scream, a woman yelling at a policeman and doctors, blips of machines and code calls.

"When I'm in pain, sometimes God helps take my mind off of it when I sing," my sister-in-law, Vangie, told Dad. She took his hand and started in on the old hymn, "What a Friend We Have in Jesus."

Suddenly, that gruff croaking voice joined hers—we had had no idea he knew that song. As Dad sang about his friend, Jesus, his restlessness abated and his soul found peace and reassurance. Three weeks later, Dad met his friend face to face. Dad discovered during that Christmas season what some people know for much of their lives—the power and comfort of a friendship with Jesus.

According to a June 2006 survey by the Barna Group, 51 percent of Americans say their Christian faith has not just affected them, but has actually transformed their lives. That's what this book is about: Firsthand accounts by Americans, and others, whose lives changed when they decided to see what the Christian religion and Jesus Christ are all about. These everyday people come from all walks and demographic categories of life, were at various ages when they sought God, and came to God in different ways.

But they all, like my dad, found the peace their souls longed for. And they discovered that Jesus Christ was not just a person who lived in history, but someone they could have a relationship with today. May you be challenged and inspired as you read their stories.

∼ Jeanette Gardner Littleton

Like Son, Like Father

"DAD, I'M GONNA be okay. I've found God! I've become a born-again Christian." Steve's excitement exploded through the phone line. My wife Barbara and I had worried about Steve, the one of our six children who had floundered around trying to "find himself." Now the alarm bells sounded loud and clear. Had Steve become involved with a cult?

Barb and I had taught our children by example that attending church was the right thing to do. However, despite my church attendance and volunteer work there, God always seemed distant to me. After the kids were grown, I slowly drifted out of the church routine. I rationalized that since I wasn't getting anything out of going, there wasn't any real reason to go. Although Barbara didn't feel that close to God herself, she had continued to attend services alone.

Barb and I discussed Steve's pronouncement. I quickly made a decision: "We'd better go visit him and see what's going on."

A few days later we arrived in Las Vegas, where Steve lived. He immediately took us to his new church. I entered the building with my internal defenses raised, only to have them crumble as I watched in amazement. In all my years spent attending church, I'd never seen such sincerity in people as they prayed and worshiped God. I wanted whatever these people had. Steve explained to Barb and me that to be assured of eternal life with God, we needed to repent of our sins and receive Christ into our hearts.

Then the most amazing thing happened. I suddenly realized that this was what I'd been missing. I'd always understood I was a sinner, but I'd never grasped that what Christ did for me on the cross I could never do for myself—atone for my sins. I'd spent years trying to do that by going to church and volunteering there. Yet I'd never succeeded in earning my own salvation.

God was working on Barb's heart at the same time, and together we prayed to receive Jesus into our hearts. When we flew home a few days later, our spirits were so high we hardly needed a plane, and we couldn't wait to tell our family the good news so they too could know Jesus.

Soon after we returned to our home in Illinois, my dad began showing signs of Alzheimer's disease. Caring for him became more and more difficult for Mom. I urged her to receive Christ and give Dad over to the Lord. God opened her heart, and before long she prayed to receive Jesus. Then my family got another shock. Mom was diagnosed with advanced cirrhosis of the liver. She died just six weeks later. Knowing she had gone to be with Jesus helped me accept her death a little more easily.

Alzheimer's disease is no respecter of family circumstance. As we grieved the loss of my mom, the illness continued to rob my dad, who was now in a nursing home, of his mind and sense of purpose. We weren't even sure he realized Mom was gone. Although I'd shared Christ with Dad before Alzheimer's invaded his life, he'd resisted the message, and this gnawed at me.

Several months later, I had lunch with a Christian friend. Over dessert, I expressed my deepest desire. "I wish I could have one more opportunity to talk with my dad about God," I said.

My friend looked me in the eye. "Maybe you can. Why not take him to the nursing-home chapel, place your hands on his head, and ask God to give him clarity of mind?"

At first the suggestion sounded like an impossible dream, but Jesus' words from Matthew, "With God all things are possible," showed me that as far as God is concerned, nothing is out of reach. I needed to step out in faith and go for it.

By the time I arrived at the nursing home a few days later, excitement over what might happen filled every part of my being. When I saw him, Dad offered me his usual childlike smile. Did the greeting mean he knew who I was? Probably not. For months, he had shown not even a glimmer of recognition at seeing my siblings or me. Today I prayed for a miracle.

I carefully led him out of the small room. "This way, Dad. Let's take a walk."

As we strolled down the well-lit hall toward the nursing-home chapel, I slowed my pace to match the old man's shuffle. The only sound in the corridor was my voice as I rambled about the latest family news, how the weather had turned cool—whatever came to mind. A familiar sadness overshadowed my heart as I chattered. How had it come to this: my dad, living his final years in this institution. No matter how nice the staff was or how well decorated and clean they kept the rooms, it was still not a home. Perhaps it was just as well that Dad seemed unaware of his surroundings.

As we entered the chapel, I breathed a sigh of relief. The room was empty. We passed several rows of straight-back chairs, all facing a simple altar-like table, and I helped Dad sit in the front row. I took the chair next to his and turned to look at him, startled at how frail he'd become. He slumped against the chair back and let his head droop until his chin rested against his chest. Where was his mind?

I took a deep breath and whispered a prayer, asking God for help. Then I gently placed my hands on top of Dad's thinning hair. "Lord, please give me the opportunity to tell Dad about You. Give him the clarity of mind necessary to understand my words."

Suddenly Dad lifted his head and looked directly at me with watery gray eyes. "Hi, Frank. How are ya?" His voice was clear and resonant.

I almost jumped out of my skin and immediately breathed a prayer of praise and thanks.

Dad looked around the room. "Mom's not here is she? She died, didn't she?"

Tears filled my eyes, and I tried to blink them away. "Yeah, but she's in heaven, and if you want to go there too, I can tell you how."

I told him about my new faith in God and how Mom accepted Christ before she died. I then explained as gently as possible that if he repented for his sins and gave his heart to Jesus, just as Mom and I had, he could go to heaven too.

"I want to do that," Dad said, nodding his head.

I gripped his hand. Hoping my voice didn't shake too much, I began the same prayer Steve had led Barb and me through a few months earlier. Dad repeated the words, confessing his sin and making a commitment to Jesus.

We both said "Amen" together, and a grin stretched across my father's face. "Now I know I'll go to heaven and be with my wife and God."

Then I watched in astonishment as Dad's chin sagged until it again rested against his chest. I looked into his eyes—they were vacant again.

I helped Dad to his feet and led him back to his room. I would have liked to have enjoyed a few more moments with the "old" dad, but then it hit me: The old dad was no more. Now, thanks to answered prayer, he was a new man in Christ. I felt as though I were walking five feet off the ground. Barb and I thought we'd hit the *true* jackpot on our trip to Vegas, when our son led us to Christ, but what had just happened really took the prize!

Dad never again recognized anyone or held a rational conversation. The following Thanksgiving Day, he died. I could only rejoice and thank God. What had happened that day in that nursing home was a miracle only God could have performed. Dad was in heaven with his wife and his God, and I had learned a valuable lesson: Never doubt God or hesitate to step out in faith. Nothing is impossible with God. Absolutely nothing.

~ *Frank Coppaletta, as told to Pam Meyers*

Dirty Laundry

THE LAUNDRY BASKET bumped against my hip with each step leading down to the first floor of my apartment building, where a washer and dryer sat side by side under a bare light bulb. I dug into my jeans pocket for three quarters. Laundry. That was my routine every Friday night while my friends were having fun at the movies. A series of regrettable choices had left me married to an alcoholic, with the heavy responsibility of raising our two-year-old daughter. And I was only twenty-one.

I stared blankly into the washer's tub as it filled. Thoughts about my life and how I'd ended up this way crowded against each other as I sprinkled detergent into the water. It wasn't supposed to be like this. I was supposed to be happy.

I dumped the jumble of socks and T-shirts into the murky water, hesitating when I came to my favorite blue shirt. I fingered its softness and remembered when another favorite shirt had disappeared from this very machine a few weeks earlier. I guessed some of my neighbors thought nothing of sneaking downstairs to take whatever clothing they chose from a full washer or dryer and claiming it as their own. I sighed and tossed the dirty shirt into the washer.

Back in the quiet apartment, I checked on my sleeping daughter and settled on the sofa's thin cushion with nothing to do but wait for the rinse cycle. Weekends were always the hardest. I had nothing to do and no money to do it with. Too much time to think. At least during the week, I had a job to escape to. And Susan was there.

Even though I'd only known Susan three months, already I thought of the petite redhead as one of my best friends. She was fun and smart, and she genuinely cared about me. We had only gone to lunch a couple of times before she'd tenderly brought up my need for God.

I had brushed the crumbs off my lap and chuckled. "Oh, Susan! I'm already a Christian! My mom says I asked Jesus into my heart when I was three years old. I've been saved almost all my life!"

But I admired Susan for having the courage to do something I never do—witness.

I liked knowing Susan was a Christian like me. We spent nearly every lunch hour together and talked for hours. Susan's favorite topic of conversation was always Jesus. Usually, I could take only so much of that, but listening to Susan was different. Her hazel eyes sparkled when she told me of yet another amazing thing she discovered about Him. She said He even made her laugh!

Susan's Jesus intrigued me. He was so much more to her than what He'd always been to me—a bearded face in a picture frame. One night Susan came to my place and we talked for hours, as I'd told her about every wrong thing I'd ever done. I thought my mistakes and sins were too much for even Jesus to overlook. I figured that's why He couldn't be to me what He was to Susan. But she assured me I was mistaken, telling me about her own errors.

Even after that night ended, I kept thinking about her words, the tears she cried on my behalf, and her parting prayer for me. I thought about how real Jesus was to Susan, how she acted as if she really knew Him, and how she spoke of Him as if He was her best friend. Susan was in love, and I was jealous.

I jumped off the sofa, suddenly unable to sit still as frustration, doubt, guilt, longing, fear, and anger fought inside me as I headed to the kitchen for a glass of water. Why was this so hard for me? I'd been taught about God all my life. My mom knew more Bible verses by memory than anybody. I had spent every Sunday morning, Sunday night, and Wednesday night in church for my entire childhood. At age ten, I knew the books of the Bible by heart. If anyone knew what it took to be a Christian, it was me. So why did I feel like I didn't know Jesus at all? Why was I scared of Him? Why did thinking about Him make me feel guilty?

I set my empty glass on the counter and looked at my watch, realizing the clothes should be ready for the dryer. I checked my pocket for quarters and headed to the first floor, trying to get a handle on my emotions. Surprisingly, anger had shouldered its way to the front of my emotional line, and I began tugging wet clothes from the machine with an unnecessary amount of force. *Why can't I understand? Why can't I accept God's love for me? Is there something wrong with me? Why is it so easy for Susan to love God and accept His love for her in return, while all I want to do is hide? How can she run to Him with open arms, when my first response to His nearness is to duck?*

My anger escalated, and I wanted to throw something. I vaguely heard the people moving around in the rooms above my head, but no one entered the hallway. I stopped, alone on the first floor with my daughter's damp, pink sundress in my hands.

Unsure of what I was about to do, my eyes went to the ceiling and settled on a water stain that looked like California. I didn't even realize my feet were planted hip-distance apart and my shoulders were back, as if I were getting ready to take on the laundry phantom who had swiped my favorite T-shirt. And before I knew it, I said what I've wanted to say for years.

"God? I've made a mess of my life. If you can do better, it's yours. Take my life and make something good out of it." I flung the pink dress into the dryer and slammed the door. My eyes fastened on California. "And I'll know you're real if my life starts to change."

My legs felt weak as I climbed the stairs. "What in the world have I done?" I murmured. Had I just committed the unpardonable sin? Had I just challenged God? Had I dared the Creator of the Universe to love me? Then why didn't I feel guilty or ashamed of myself?

I should feel something, shouldn't I? I wondered.

I sat gingerly on the sofa, realizing I did indeed feel something. For the first time that I could remember, I felt *heard*.

As I dressed for work Monday morning, I thought of what I'd say to Susan. Nothing out of the ordinary had happened during the rest of the weekend. I was determined that above all, I wouldn't let myself be fooled into believing something that wasn't really there. I planned to double-check every feeling or thought I had. This was going to be for real, or it wasn't going to be at all.

Susan and I met for lunch as usual, and I let her take a few bites of her sandwich before I told her about my one-sided conversation with God. Her eyes lit up and her smile glowed. As I told her about the experience, and of the sense that God had really heard me, I couldn't help but feel a little excited myself.

My day-to-day life changed little over the next month. I was still married to a man who got his paycheck at five o'clock every Friday and had drunk half of it by midnight. I was still, for all practical purposes, a single parent to my little girl. But now I was more interested than ever in the things Susan talked about. She showed me something in the Bible, and I wanted to read it too. When I prayed, I discover myself simply talking to Jesus, not following a script. Slowly, I became more comfortable telling Him things—my needs, my wants, my fears, and my dreams for the future.

The warm months of summer were nearly over and a definite crispness filled the air, especially in the mornings as I drove to work. I braked for a red light and thought about my goals for the weekend. It was time to get out last year's winter clothes and see what would still fit my growing two-year-old. I would have to replace whatever didn't. But I had to pay the rent first. How could I ever manage it all on my tight budget?

All Saturday afternoon I coaxed my uncooperative daughter in and out of those old clothes. Most things were snug, but the pajamas were way too small. When the fashion show ended, I determined the clothing I'd need to buy and estimated the cost. My heart sunk when I realized I simply didn't have enough money for everything. Several evenings of frugal shopping confirmed my worries when I returned home with the bare necessities—and no pajamas.

Tell Jesus. The thought dropped into my mind like a coin into a slot. Why not? I lowered myself to the edge of the bed.

"Jesus," I whispered, "my little girl needs pajamas. I know she could use her old ones for a while, but if . . ."

A solid knock at the apartment door interrupted me. When I opened the door, I recognized the woman who lived across the hall. Not knowing her name, I simply smiled. "Yes?"

And then I saw it. I barely heard her words of explanation, of how her daughter only wore it twice, of how she'd outgrown it so fast, and wasn't my daughter about this size? My eyes were riveted to the white cotton nightgown she held out, the fabric sprinkled with pink roses. The gown, draped over a hanger, even had a matching robe.

I stammered a thank-you, too stunned to say more. I closed the door and stood in the silence of the living room, unable to take my eyes from the miracle in my hand. And in that moment, I knew.

Jesus was real. Everything the Bible said about Him was true. Not only that, but He knew who I was. He loved my little girl and me. And He had just proved it.

I hugged the gown and buried my face in its folds, letting the tears come. On the bottom floor of an apartment building, I had thrust my chin at God. And He had seen me there, with my dirty laundry, trying to make clean what would only become soiled again. He had been there all along, waiting for me. And one reluctant *yes* was all it had taken for Him to pour His living water over my heart, cleansing my soul forever.

~ *Cynthia L. D'Agostino*

Fighting the Good Fight

I TASTED THE blood on my cut lip and smelled the sweat of my own fear. The roar of the crowd faded beneath the sound of my own racing heartbeat and the grunt of my opponent as I landed the next brutal blow. I knew about the Christian ideal of turning the other cheek, but that was not for me. I was a fighter.

My name is Somchai—"macho man." As a Muay Thai kickboxer, my duty was to deal out and counteract lethal blows, aiming at victory and ruining the career of the opponent in the ring. The satisfaction of delivering vicious, lightning-fast punishment was one way to overcome my own body's agony after the match was fought and won. I owed it to myself, my reputation, and my hordes of faithful admirers to obtain victory. I rode high on the waves of their supportive cheers and the excitement I generated as I contended in furious battles of brawn and wits. And I paid my fans back handsomely with the huge amounts of money they made when I won. Yes, I was invulnerable.

After the match, I felt their love and concern over my bruises as I jumped from the ring and they touched me for luck. Often hurting badly, I'd stagger only later, when no one could see. It didn't matter if the pain made me sick to my stomach, for soon these good fellows would take me out to the best of Bangkok's nightclubs. They would ply me with liquor to dull the soreness of my ribs and the stiffness of my battered thighs. After all, I was the triumphant warrior straight from a glorious battle, or so they continually assured me.

I don't know why it never occurred to me that while they were getting richer and fatter, I was suffering more and more. But popularity is a strong drug; a little is not enough. I was proof to them of what it meant to be a real man. I was making good money, too, and one day I'd buy a big home and a flashy car. I would be on equal footing with a man who deals in gold jewelry. I would also have my pick of all those beautiful girls we Thais are so proud of.

After recuperating from my battle scars, the rigorous training sessions would begin again. But after each match, I noticed it was becoming more difficult to gain peak physical condition. Somehow I never realized that the drinking, smoking, and carousing were softening me up for something more painful.

One night after a long session with my warm-hearted friends, I doubled over in an agony that would not quit. I cannot remember much of it, but my parents took me to the nearby Bangkok Christian Hospital. I saw their anxious faces as I moved in and out of consciousness. I had stomach ulcer perforations, they told me. They said something like, "The doctors operated on you, but don't worry; you are young. You can start over again." Even through my pain, I thought I would fight again. I believed in myself. Pain was not something new to me. My career was my life!

But the fighting spirit began to leave me as dreary day followed day, and I was confined to my hospital bed, wondering why my friends weren't surrounding me. Each day I invented new excuses for their absence, until finally the bitter truth sank in like the venom of a cobra strike: They didn't care. Even now they'd be fawning over other young hopefuls. While I lay there, helpless and friendless, they were surely enjoying themselves and getting even richer. A heavy blanket of depression settled over me. I sank so low I didn't care if I died. My life was over anyway. The fight was gone.

Right there, at the point of my deepest need, God stepped into the ring of my life. A small group of young Christians from a nearby church visited the hospital to say hello to patients and sing a few cheerful Christian songs. Some of them even told about their relationships with God. They were around my own age, and their faces radiated their belief in their Jesus. I had never seen or heard anything like it before. I listened closely to everything they said.

They didn't need to convince me I was a sinner—I knew I needed a Savior, and I responded immediately when they asked if anyone wanted to have a relationship with Jesus. And after I asked Jesus into my life, the great weights of disappointment, frustration, and bitterness left me. I felt as fine as I always had in the ring before a match.

When I left the hospital, my old "friends" weren't interested in the change of direction in my life. They considered Christianity a Western religion, and I think they sensed that I'd lost my desire to reach the heights of the boxing sphere at any cost. Instead, God had replaced that fighting energy with a hunger for spiritual things. Needing some new guidelines to follow in this new life ring, I began to go to the same church as the young people who had visited the hospital. I still didn't understand so much, so I decided to attend Bible college and learn more about this whole new Christian experience.

The next step after that seemed a natural one. Because I was proficient in English, some missionaries asked me to teach them the Thai language and customs. Some time later, a member of the Pocket Testament League challenged me to join their organization in distributing tens of thousands of copies of the Gospel of John translated into Thai.

I met my dear wife, Saenthong, in Phuket while I was ministering. She gave me two fine sons who are now old enough to enable her to travel with me. Saenthong was raised by missionaries and became a schoolteacher. Now she ministers in women's and children's meetings and regularly writes to people who want to learn more about Jesus through a correspondence course. We also interpret for evangelists from other countries when they visit our country. And we were deeply touched when large church groups from America came to help our tsunami-ravaged coastline. Some of those Christians were doctors and nurses who ministered to our many orphans.

Our king, Rama IX, is the "Defender of the Faiths" — *faiths*, plural — so our choice of religion is not restricted by politics. Because I belong to the Evangelical Churches of Thailand, I am certified by the government to share Christianity at any institution where people have a willingness or an interest to hear the message I present. Because of this, many doors are opened to me. I can freely enter government Buddhist schools, hospitals, prisons, and even marketplaces. Buddhists will listen to anyone, so it is even easier for them to hear the true Gospel. Although they will not stand for anyone denigrating Buddha, there is no need for me to take jabs at their beliefs. I simply uplift Jesus by explaining His sacrifice. Our land has a mix of many other races and belief systems, which are based on the existence of both good and evil spirits who must constantly be appeased. Miniature spirit houses, for placatory offerings of food or flowers, are built outside homes, schools, businesses, and shopping malls. It's a wonderful ring in which to defend the faith and champion Jesus.

Because there is such great need, I have never lost my excitement and enthusiasm for telling my people about Jesus; for offering them the salvation that depends on faith in Him alone; and for sharing with them that unlike our national religion of Buddhism, Jesus promises joy right here on earth as well as the surety of one day having a home in heaven for eternity. I feel the same enthusiasm and adrenaline for this fighting in the spiritual realm as I did when I was fighting earthly contenders.

And so, the work that Jesus began in me—a champion who once thought he had the world at his feet—continues. Once I fought for prizes and fame; now I fight for faith, so others may receive the prize of the high calling of God in Christ Jesus!

> ∼ *Somchai Soonthornturasuk,*
> *as told to Rita Stella Galieh*

Born Again? Oh No!

"Won't you please come to church with me today, Mom? It's Easter Sunday," my daughter, Mary Beth, pleaded as she stood at my bedroom door.

I had been to a party the night before, so I just groaned. "I have a headache." I didn't want to go to church that day, or any day—especially not to *that* church.

Mary Beth was fifteen years old when she became, of all things, a born-again Christian.

"Born again?" I had silently cried. "Oh, no!" As a single mom raising my kids alone, I worried about this new turn of events in my daughter's life. During the next few months, I waited for her to lose interest in this strange new fanaticism. But as time passed and she became more involved with her new church, I grew increasingly concerned.

Plenty of hippies live in Southern California, and it was hippies who came to our home to take my daughter to church. They arrived in a van hand-painted with flowers, its sides emblazoned with slogans such as "Jesus Lives!" "One Way," and "Hallelujah, the Lord is coming soon!"

Mary Beth would come home from the church meetings and exclaim, "Oh, Mom, you really should visit this church. The youth leader looks like Jesus. And they have rock bands that play right in the church. It's *sooo* neat!" That description did nothing to allay my worries.

Time passed, and for the first time my daughter and I were not getting along. Although she radiated a new softness and sweetness, she would say things like, "Mom, you're going to hell if you don't accept Jesus." She even said that I would have to go through "the Tribulation," whatever that was.

I knew I would have to do something. She was obviously not outgrowing this phase that was creating so much friction. I decided I would visit her church to see just what kind of a cult she had gotten into. I would explain to her what was wrong with it. And after that, I would no longer let her attend church there. So one balmy April evening, Mary Beth and I headed to "cult headquarters"—but only after I had fortified myself with a vodka tonic.

As we approached the church, I could hardly believe my eyes. Cars were parked for blocks around this little chapel. *Are all these people going to church?* I wondered. *It isn't even Sunday.*

With its beige stucco walls, red-tiled roof, and arched doorways, the building stood like a Spanish mission in the middle of a bean field, with scores of young people flowing toward it. We couldn't find a parking place nearby and had to walk a couple of long blocks to reach the church. Now I could see why my daughter had insisted that we arrive an hour early.

The church courtyard was filled with hundreds of kids, all dressed like hippies. Some of the kids wore "love beads" or huge wooden crosses on leather necklaces. Some had little wire-rimmed glasses perched on their noses. Several wore sandals and others were barefoot. But they all wore huge smiles.

My apprehension faded. *I've never seen so many happy faces at church,* I thought. Kids hugged and greeted each other enthusiastically. They were shouting things like, "Praise the Lord," "God bless you," and "Far out, sister! Glad you're here!"

When we went inside, the rock band started to play, and all the kids began to sing. The atmosphere of love was so thick you could feel it in the air, and it settled around me like a soft, warm blanket. An ethereal glow filled the place. In that moment, I knew! This was not a cult, but the real thing—an alive and loving church.

The name of the church was Calvary Chapel, and a man named Chuck Smith was its senior pastor. It was one of the first churches to reach out to the flower children and other youth in the drug culture. This came to be known as the Jesus Movement.

I loved it! I loved all of it that night: the sweet, loving, friendly kids; the youth leader who looked like Jesus; and the rock band called Love Song. With tears in my eyes, I settled into my seat and let the love flow over me.

The message that night, delivered by the buckskin-clad, hippie preacher, was simple, direct, and dynamic. He spoke about the love of God and about the saving grace of His Son, Jesus.

After attending meetings there for a short time, I rededicated my life to the Lord, and Calvary Chapel became my church, too. Our home became peaceful, and my daughter became my best friend. I stopped searching for fulfillment in all the wrong places and in wrong relationships. I finally found the joy and peace, which I had been searching for all my life, in my walk with Jesus. "Old things are passed away . . . all things are become new" (2 Corinthians 5:17).

Thank you, Lord, that you used my daughter to lead me back to you. And thanks for showing me what being born again really means: a lifelong walk as a new person, with Jesus at the center of my life.

Born again? Oh yes!

$\sim$ *Gay Sorensen*

A Worthwhile Life

"TOM LACY, DON'T you think it's about time you did something worthwhile with your life?" Earl Butler, my coworker, blocked my path to the sales manager's office and poked the middle of my chest with his index finger. This wasn't the first time. I knew Earl was a Christian and wanted to start a conversation so he could preach at me.

Auto salesmen develop quick comebacks, so I had one ready. "I'm selling lots of cars, making big bucks, wearing nice clothes, eating good food, drinking good booze, and taking care of my family better than ever before. I *am* doing something worthwhile with my life," I shot back.

But it bothered me that Earl would demand an answer to such a question. His plea seemed urgent and forceful, and it made me feel defensive. Who did Earl think he was? After all, he knew I took my wife and five children to Sunday school and church every time the doors were open. Wasn't that worth something? Why was he being so pushy? I brushed his hand aside, and went to get my deal approved. That was the worthwhile thing to do at the moment—not answer Earl's probing question.

My response probably didn't satisfy Earl because he knew the other side of my lifestyle, too. I was an alcoholic. I was always either getting drunk, in the middle of being drunk, or sobering up from being drunk. I eventually reached the height—or depth—of my drinking. I wasn't chemically addicted to the drug alcohol, but I was emotionally dependent upon it. Alcohol is a depressant, and takes a heavy toll on the body and the brain. I became openly depressed. A person's life runs on four tires: physical, mental, emotional, and spiritual. During that time of my life I was running on four flat tires.

I couldn't blame my drinking on my past. As a child, I had gone to Sunday school and church. I filled my blue-ribbon attendance awards with gold stars for learning Bible verses and winning Bible drills. But no change took place in my heart or in my life. In fact, I dropped out of Sunday school and church when I was fourteen. I drank my first beer at seventeen—that's when I got hooked.

But just because I was hooked didn't mean I was a bum. Didn't Earl realize that? I *was* doing something worthwhile. Couldn't he see that? I had always been a hard worker. I worked every day. With every job I'd ever had, I'd started at the bottom and worked my way up to the top, or else I'd left for a better position.

In fact, I had earned top dollar in the printing industry. To earn any more, I would have had to travel, and I didn't want to be away from my kids that much. So, after thirteen years in the printing field, I got a salesman's job at the large auto dealership where my brother-in-law worked.

I had taken a couple of weeks off before starting my new position, thinking the break would rejuvenate me. It didn't. I became depressed to the point of being suicidal. I believed my family would be better off without me and planned to take my own life on June 27, a day when I knew no one else would be home.

At ten o'clock that morning, I started to stand up from the sofa to get a sharp butcher knife from the kitchen. But I felt an unexplainable force pressing on the top of my head. It literally drove me to my knees. Without hesitation, I prayed, "Lord, I don't know why you would listen to someone like me; but I pray you will bless me and prosper me. Amen."

Void of emotion, even after I prayed, I got off my knees and resumed my normal routine—that is, if you can describe an alcoholic's life as normal. Nothing seemed to have changed. I was still depressed, but I was still alive. I went to my new job.

Selling cars was an exciting challenge, and I excelled at it. In the first six months on the job, my income more than doubled. Rather than show gratitude to God for prospering me, I began drinking better booze. Alcohol consumed more and more of my life. But that didn't stop God from working on me.

December isn't the best month in the automobile business. Many dealerships offer incentives in December to generate sales. That year, to increase competition, our sales force was divided into teams. The dealership offered a free beef 'n' booze dinner—all you could eat and drink—to the winning sales team. That was my kind of party, and my team won the honors.

On the big night, I volunteered to set up the dining hall—not because I was Mr. Nice Guy, but so I could get into the booze an hour earlier. By the time I had everything in place, I was drinking my second double bourbon and water.

I set my drink on the table in front of me to light a cigarette. In that instant, God made His move. I've heard that on the brink of death, people's lives flash before their eyes.

Suddenly God showed me my life as He saw it. Seventeen years of drunken debauchery rolled past my mind's eye.

As I stood frozen in that moment, Earl's words echoed in my mind. "Tom Lacy, don't you think it's about time you did something worthwhile with your life?"

Did Earl have some sort of premonition of things to come in my life? Did God cause him to be so pushy that day? Was God trying to tell me something?

Earl's words took on new meaning. As the blinders fell from my eyes, I said to myself, "I don't want to live this way another day."

Then, as quickly as it had happened, the experience was over. I looked at the table. Sitting beside my drink was a cup of coffee I knew I hadn't put there. Coffee was for sobering up. Extinguishing the match, I looked from the bourbon to the coffee and back. I knew I had to make a critical decision—one that would affect me, and everyone in my life, from that moment into eternity. So I made my choice. I picked up the coffee. I went home sober that night for the first time in many years.

I have reviewed that crucial event in the dining hall many times in my life, and I believe it was then that God saved me. At the snap of His finger, the Almighty delivered me from the sin of alcoholism and the control it held over me. He reversed my prayer—He prospered me and *then* blessed me. He heard my cry for help as a cry for salvation.

After not drinking for six weeks, I told my family, "I don't think I'm going to drink anymore." But I couldn't make a firm commitment. Too many times I'd uttered these same words, only to get drunk again.

"Why should we believe you this time?" they asked.

This question was like Earl's. It could've angered me if I'd taken it as a put-down. It could've launched another drinking binge, but it didn't. I thought for a long, reflective moment before answering.

"God has given me a new attitude," I said. "For the first time in seventeen years I know drinking is wrong."

I spent four of the next seven years taking a Bible correspondence course and testing my growth and spiritual gifts by taking various jobs in the church. Those who had known me as an alcoholic began to recognize me as a changed man. My family and church supported and encouraged me in my new walk in life.

Armed with God's new attitude, at age forty-one, I accepted His call on my life into full-time ministry. After completing my seminary studies, I was ordained into the gospel ministry and appointed chaplain of the Hanover County Jail in Virginia, where I served for twelve years. During that time my wife decided she wanted out of our marriage. Despite counseling, our marriage ended. Eventually, God changed the direction of my ministry from jail chaplaincy to family crisis counseling.

When I look back, I see that Earl was just being obedient to God when he asked me that life-changing question so many years ago. Earl is with the Lord now, but his challenge still lives: *Don't you think it's about time you did something worthwhile with your life?*

~ *Rev. Thomas C. Lacy*

The School Board Meeting
That Changed My Life

WHEN I LISTEN to the various political controversies, especially the censorship and intelligent design issues that local schools debate, I remember the school board meeting that changed my life.

The year before the U.S. Supreme Court made school-sponsored prayer illegal, the school board of our small Connecticut town had already eliminated the longtime practice of starting each school day with classroom prayer. Citizen reaction to the board's edict was mixed, and feelings on both sides of the issue ran high.

I opposed the school board's action, but not on religious grounds. I wasn't a Christian. I believed that the school board was tampering with religious freedom as guaranteed by the U.S. Constitution. Others who shared my point of view banded together. We gathered hundreds of signatures from residents who also wanted to keep prayer as part of the daily opening exercises at our schools.

This committee asked me to present our petition forms to the school board at the next meeting. The room was packed to the rafters with town officials, parents, clergy, and a horde of newspaper photographers and reporters. My hands shook as I handed over our stack of petitions and made my well-practiced speech to scattered applause as well as boos. A young pastor was next to speak. I could hardly believe his calm and commitment as he not only spoke in favor of prayer but also asked the board to add Bible reading to the schools' program! Reporters scribbled furiously, and photographers snapped his picture. The school board overruled our petitions and requests, but the young pastor's courage made him my hero that night.

Several weeks later, I saw an ad for something called "Vacation Bible School," which offered free bus transportation to a weekday children's program that lasted two full weeks. The church, I realized, was led by the same young pastor. My husband and I weren't churchgoers, and I didn't know anything about this children's program, but I trusted the pastor. The next week, all three of my children were on the bus.

Again, this was not a religious decision—I just wanted some rest. My husband had nearly died from a bleeding ulcer and was sent home from the hospital with the orders to stay calm and quiet. Try to follow those instructions with a fourteen-year-old boy and two girls aged five and nine running around! The thought of some shut-eye—rather than any desire to have my kids learn the Bible—inspired me to enroll them.

I was shocked when the kids all seemed to enjoy themselves. A Friday night closing session was scheduled at the end of the two weeks, and the children begged me to attend. I didn't want to go. Listening to a bunch of kids recite unfamiliar Bible verses wasn't my idea of an exciting Friday night. But it was important to my children, and my husband was even feeling well enough to attend as well.

What a surprise was in store for us! All of the children, including our own, were well behaved as they sang Bible-based songs and recited Scripture verses. We were both impressed with what we saw. We sensed that something special was going on at that church.

After the kids' program, we chatted with other parents and some of the church leaders, including the pastor. To my surprise, they all seemed like regular people, not super religious or condescending toward those who didn't go to church.

On the way home, I grumbled as the children begged us to take them to Sunday school that weekend. I imagined the craziness of getting my tribe fed and dressed in time for the 9:30 A.M. classes instead of enjoying my usual leisurely Sunday morning. But I couldn't resist my children's pleas. *It's not as if they're asking to do something bad,* I told myself.

The first couple of Sundays, I dropped the kids off and went to a doughnut shop across the street. A few weeks later, a church member invited me to the adult class that met at the same time. I decided to try it. It was certainly cheaper and a lot less fattening than the doughnut shop!

At that first class, I was fascinated that so many normal-looking people were interested in studying the Bible and were even memorizing a scripture verse each month. If thirty or forty people my age or older were that serious about the Bible, I thought, maybe I should investigate it, too. But following through on that initial curiosity was another story. I don't know how long I would have procrastinated if I hadn't encountered a family crisis.

With my husband still unable to work, we started facing serious financial problems and fell behind in our mortgage payments. Worse yet, our marriage was deteriorating faster than our credit rating. I didn't know how to deal with my feelings, short of pounding my head against the wall. I knew I had to take some kind of action. But what?

An answer tiptoed into my mind: *Pray.* It seemed like a great solution. Hadn't I fought to keep prayer in the classroom? But I found that thinking about praying and actually praying were two different things. Beyond reciting the Lord's Prayer, which I had learned as a child, I didn't know how to pray. I remember sitting at my kitchen table, drinking coffee and feeling helpless, when I thought about looking for help in the Bible. Someone had given me one, but I wasn't sure where it was. I rummaged through my bedroom drawers until I found it.

My next problem was figuring out where in the Bible to find help. A table of contents listed the names of the books and where to locate them, but that was little help to someone who didn't know what was in their books. Finally I thought of an avenue that was open to me—the pastor. Perhaps he'd help me with the questions that swirled through my mind.

I was sitting in his office an hour later, my eyes drawn to a huge painting on one wall. It showed a mass of humanity on one side of a wide chasm and a peaceful heavenly scene on the other side. A huge wooden cross stretched across the chasm, from one cliff to the other. The pastor explained that the cross represented Jesus Christ, who died on the cross to bring us into relationship with God. I didn't understand the theology, but something inside me told me I needed Jesus in my life. I followed the pastor in a prayer, asking Jesus to wash away the sins of my past life and make me new. I was confident that Jesus had heard me because I felt truly clean and new inside.

For the next several months, I devoured the Bible. I couldn't seem to get enough of it. And I began to pray every day, starting with simple sentence prayers in which I told God I loved Him and needed His help. As I grew in my new faith, God gave me peace about the future. The situations in my life were still difficult, but now I trusted that God would help me. I wasn't the least bit upset when we had to move to a less expensive home to get our finances back in order. Over time, God melted my heart and renewed my love for my husband. Our relationship became better than ever, and within the year, my husband also became a Christian.

Having Jesus in my life gives me joy I never knew before, a deep-down confidence in a God who loves me and directs my path each day. After all, He directed me from a school board meeting room into a journey of faith.

$\sim$ *Joyce Starr Macias*

The Collision

SOMETIMES YOU BEGIN by running away. Your plan for life becomes the equivalent of driving fast and deliberately taking roads not on the map. You smile as you imagine yourself gripping the wheel, in charge of your own destiny. Nothing will keep you from success and future fame.

You firmly believe all this until the wreck.

The only illumination that night came from the reflection of headlights off snow-covered fields. My feet were on the icy two-lane highway—in front of my mangled car. I'd run a stop sign in this unfamiliar part of Washington State and been struck by a truck going sixty miles per hour. I felt a tremendous wallop, heard the lighter sound of shattering glass, and the car spun in a circle like a carnival ride.

I got out, confused. The driver of the other vehicle was holding his arm and cursing me. My brother, my only passenger, was also able to walk. He came up and looked at the side of our sedan. Everything we owned was packed tightly into the car. Some of it had been flung into the ditch by the impact. Keith looked at the car again and remarked in an awed tone that if the impact had come a few inches further forward, he would be in the hospital or dead.

I wished I could start over. I would see the intersection. I would apply the brakes. Everything would be fine again.

After all, this couldn't be happening to me. I was recently graduated from an Ivy League college, with an agent, a collection of short stories ready to sell to a New York publisher, and money in the bank from working a stretch in the oil field.

I was twenty-four and on my way, the kind of guy who could pack up on a whim and say, *I'm heading south for the winter.* Nothing mattered as long as I sought interesting people and kept on writing books. I didn't owe anything to anybody. Until this moment, I had thought I was invulnerable.

In fact, I was a prodigal.

I should have known that. The runaway son Jesus portrayed in his parable is a young man who starts out in the right place. He is with his father in his father's house. He has all the privileges. That could have described someone like me, who came from a Christian family and grew up going to church. I was baptized at thirteen, and I owned a Bible. But by the time I went off to college, I found it all too constricting. I knew a larger world existed out there, and I had to explore it.

So in my mind, I made a pact with God. I would abandon Him until I reached age thirty. Then I would dust off my Bible, read it from beginning to end, and obey whatever appeared true.

In this respect I was like many in my generation. Growing up, we spent Sundays in church, yet often we never met Jesus. Church was polite social interaction, and by the time I was a teen it hardly seemed relevant. I was part of an idealistic group that wanted equal rights for everyone and no war. Most of all, we were impatient. Politics would do the job. If not that, revolution.

It didn't occur to people like me that if we wanted to change the world, we should start by letting God change us. Like the prodigal, I demanded my inheritance so I could leave for the distant country and invent my own life.

In college I lived beside interesting sinners—part-time partiers and full-time utilitarians. They believed life was about looking out for themselves and getting a sequence of degrees so they could become high-paid professionals. My friends didn't have an inkling that there was another way to live.

This was a revelation for someone who had grown up around Christians, who at least outwardly tried to be unselfish. Even as I sat beside my peers and earned their approval by doing what they did, I pretended I was different. After all, deep down I still believed in God. I also knew God could forgive, and I assumed He would do so for me. I was just taking time off, becoming less naïve, familiarizing myself with the wider world I had been sheltered from. I was actually improving myself.

Prodigals always have good reasons. But there comes a time when the damage a person does is immune to rationalizations.

That crunching metal had damaged me emotionally, and post-wreck I was totaled. Keith and I covered the giant hole in the car with duct tape and plastic and determined to journey on, but I was as dented as that car. My only hope was to reach California, land of sunny beaches and a girl who was the object of my current romantic fantasies. I'd court her for a month or so and see what happened. Maybe she'd fall in love with me and somehow everything would right itself.

Everything started out according to plan. "Hello," I said, standing on her porch and pointing at my car parked out front. "I had a little accident."

She was as blond as I remembered, quiet and intelligent. I knew this would work. She would see me as heroic, a guy who took chances.

"You're lucky to be alive," she said. Then she invited me to a gospel meeting. I'd forgotten—she was still serious about religion.

If I was bored by traditional church, I was even less enthusiastic about what I considered a modern-day religious tent show, featuring a big-haired preacher prancing back and forth. This was a three-night meeting, and for the first two nights, I focused on questionable things the evangelist said. He justified owning a personal jet: "God's people travel first class!" He claimed a "vision from God" and offered a vivid account of what it had been like when God placed the breath of life into Adam.

It sounded to me like someone blowing up an air mattress. Though I felt safely superior, and hopeful that I was impressing this girl with my openness, listening to the preacher did make me wonder how I could consider myself a Christian when I lived the way I did. This girl had given me a Bible, and I had felt strange holding it on the bus on the way to the meeting, worried that people would see me with it. I had tried to keep it out of sight. Wasn't that being ashamed of Jesus?

Then I remembered my plan. God still owed me six more years.

On the last night of the gospel meeting, the altar call was issued just like before. But suddenly the reality of it struck me with force. It didn't matter if the evangelist was a charlatan, a prophet, or some combination of both. It was the *call* that was real. I was being asked if I believed Jesus was who He said He was.

To claim this belief privately, as I always had, meant nothing. If I really believed it, I would confess it publicly. No more hiding, no more tangents. Most of all, no more being ashamed of the one who had died for me. There was only one road if I believed, and it led to that stage.

I couldn't clearly articulate all these thoughts at the time. All I knew was that my feet started moving. I made it to the end of the row and stepped down the stairs to the arena floor. I worked my way toward the people gathering in front of the stage. I was anxious, knowing I didn't have a thing to offer except my willingness to pray for forgiveness and ask Jesus to lead my life from now on. What mattered was I was lost and now I was found. I had come home.

These thoughts sounded embarrassing and humiliating to my proud intellect. Still I moved on. I was more frightened of the wreckage behind me than what lay ahead.

The next day I placed a long-distance call. Through the phone-booth glass, I watched the burst into a tangerine sunset. I tried to explain to my parents what had happened. They were confused, having little idea of the way I had been living.

"My life is going to be different," I said. I hung up the receiver, opened the doors, and stepped out into the ocean air. There were gulls drifting in the sky above. Loose sand slipped beneath my feet. I liked how it forced me to walk slowly, deliberately. The old me would have thought that moving this way meant being mired and held back. Instead, the warm sand embraced me. It made me feel connected.

I didn't care a thing about the remaining six years on my one-sided contract with God. I was truly changed from then on. Sometimes you begin by running away. You drive fast and deliberately take roads that you think are not on the map. But no roads are unknown to God. And He signs no one-sided contracts. His love looks for us and finds us, even in the collisions of our lives.

∼ *Albert Haley*

Freedom Found

"BUT HONEY, WE know Satan is only a myth," I told my fifteen-year-old daughter. "I just can't allow you to be in a class that teaches such primitive concepts."

Samantha had attended several social events with a local church youth group, and now she wanted to join its Bible study. One look at the workbook confirmed my worst fears. This group believed in the Bible literally, not in the more evolved, metaphysical way I had been teaching her.

"I'm sorry, Samantha. I know they're nice kids, and I don't mind you going places with them. But don't let their religion rub off on you. You have to be free to find your own truth."

Samantha's shoulders dropped. She knew arguing was useless. I was too dogmatic about my beliefs—whatever they happened to be at the time—to have my mind changed.

I had spent my life searching for freedom. I sought it in liberal education, radical politics, alcohol and drugs, and sexual promiscuity. After I faced the truth about the destructiveness of drugs and alcohol, I had gotten clean and sober through a twelve-step program that introduced me to the concept of God. Before long, I began a search for more meaning—for the real spiritual truth of the world I lived in. New Age religion seemed to offer what I was looking for. I could pick from a smorgasbord of beliefs and practices to create my own custom-made spirituality. I read voraciously, studied the gurus I liked best, and attended every available New Age church, seminar, and workshop I could find.

"Honey," I reminded Samantha, "Christians don't realize that Jesus taught the same message as all of the other spiritual masters. We only need to find the god within us. Then we can create our own reality."

That's what I had been doing, after all. I was now in my second marriage, this time to a fellow seeker. Through daily meditation, affirmation, and prosperity thinking, Tripp and I had become quite successful. We owned a prosperous business and a great home. We had five children—two daughters from my first marriage, three sons from our own.

Our success attracted others, who came to us for spiritual counsel. We introduced them to the practices that had worked for us, assuring them they could find happiness, too. But when we shut the door behind them, we were left with each other and the knowledge that a flaw hid beneath the surface of our success. My husband and I, each seeming to be so in harmony with the universe, could not achieve harmony in our marriage.

When two people, each claiming godhood, try to live under the same roof, well, that's not an easy task. I only knew I was tired of the arguing, and tired of reality being so different from my ideals. I felt trapped and longed once again for freedom.

Before I could take any action, God intervened. I was flipping the car radio from station to station one morning while driving the children to school, and I heard about a conference to help strengthen marriages. Of course, I was skeptical. After all, Tripp and I considered ourselves spiritual giants, and we hadn't been able to find happiness in our marriage. How could some-one else show us?

Still, in a last-ditch effort to make our marriage succeed, I signed us up for the conference the following weekend. I figured that if it didn't work, I could in good conscience leave my husband and start a new life.

Tripp and I fought all the way to the conference. The atmosphere in our car was filled with bitterness by the time we arrived at the hotel. Looking back, I am struck by the miracle of God reaching through our spiritual darkness to bring us to a place where we would hear the truth.

On the first night of the conference, the leaders offered teachings that totally contradicted my feminist, New Age perspective. We learned how God's plan for marriage differed from the world's. Because the family is God's building block for society, the conference leaders said, it is under exceptional spiritual attack.

Something clicked in my mind. I finally had to admit that my beliefs offered no reasonable explanation for the problems in my own New Age marriage or for the evil and destruction rampant in the world around me.

The next morning, I went to the sessions like an empty pitcher, waiting to be filled. We learned that God loves us and wants us to "have peace with [Him] through our Lord Jesus Christ" (Romans 5:1). But our sin separated us from God. Even our best efforts were not enough to bridge the gap. Christ had died for our sins to bring us closer to God. It was now up to us to choose to accept Him into our lives.

I had never heard anything like this before. God was personal, and He loved me! Jesus was more than a spiritual master!

I prayed silently, confessing my sin and my need, accepting Jesus as my Lord and my Savior. Through my tears, I looked up and saw my husband crying too. He reached over and wrapped his big, warm hand around mine, a tangible expression of the peace and protection I now sensed over my life and my marriage.

Truly we were changed when we came home. With no previous exposure to Christianity, we couldn't put a name on our experience. But because Jesus had entered our lives, we were led to change in many ways. We threw away all our New Age books and tapes. Instead, we avidly read the Bible. Finally we learned in John 3:3 that we had been born again. In that scripture, Jesus said: "I say unto thee, Except a man be born again, he cannot see the kingdom of God"

That's when I remembered the Bible study I had forbidden my daughter to attend. That church would probably be the right place for us after all! We entered there as mere babes in the spiritual realm, not as the highly evolved spiritual beings we had once thought ourselves to be.

"What are they into now?" our children, our parents, and our friends asked. Those who knew me well and who knew my lust for freedom were especially skeptical. They thought Christianity would be just another fad for me to explore before moving to something new. But it was just the beginning. At church we began to study the Bible in earnest—and not just the quotes that New Age teachers had pulled out to make their own points. Christian families took us under their wings, inviting us over for meals and conversation. They called this "discipling" and "fellowship." We called it learning and love. Because Tripp and I had not come from Christian backgrounds, we loved being in the company of families who'd known Christ for generations.

We were attracted by the feelings of security and peace we felt in their homes. We wanted that, too.

And so we worked a little harder, sensing that God had done something very special in bringing us into a relationship with him. Even though we were not Christians when we married, Tripp and I knew that God had been working in our lives even before we came to know Him personally. With a total of five children already—hopefully with more to come—we saw that we were in a position to change our family's legacy for future generations. That was exciting!

The developments over the next months were also exciting. When we found out that our oldest daughter and her boyfriend, both seventeen years old, were sexually involved, we shared the Good News we'd found with them. They both accepted Christ and returned to a pure relationship. They later married and now have a solid Christian family with five children. Our second daughter, then thirteen, accepted Christ a few months later. Now she too has a solid Christian family.

Eighteen years have passed, and Tripp and I are the parents of twelve. Since the birth of our eighth child, who has Down syndrome, and following our ninth, we have adopted three other babies with Down syndrome. This is something we could never have done without the love of our Heavenly Father, who first loved and adopted us into His kingdom.

Over the years, each of our other children has accepted Christ. While one has turned away from his faith, because I know so well the power of God to change lives, I am trusting God to bring him home.

No matter what changes we experience, our home has a peace that never leaves. Tripp and I still have our disagreements, but they no longer threaten our marriage or our love. In the past, each of us despised the other for being different. Now we see that God has a special plan for our lives together. We need each other to make sound decisions, and above all we need God.

As for me, I'm still a spiritual child, delighted with God. Ironically, I, who sought everywhere for that elusive state of freedom, have found it where I least expected. No longer driven by empty desires and passions, I am free to enjoy a growing relationship with God each day. I'm not searching anymore, for "where the Spirit of the Lord is, there is liberty" (2 Corinthians 3:17).

∼ Barbara Curtis

Those Who Believe

THE PERSIAN GULF sun burned brutally that Sunday morning in southeast Iraq as our Humvee bounced over the rutted streets of Safwan village.

Sergeant Vicky Vernardo gripped the steering wheel and looked at me. "Doctor Hanson, I know we have a job to do, and the villagers and our division desperately need water. But I wish we had gone to Chaplain Al's worship service before leaving base. Still would have had plenty of time to do this mission."

I gritted my teeth. "Worship service? The water recon mission is more important than early morning church."

Vernardo swallowed. "Sir, I thought you said that before the Gulf War, you went to church every Sunday when you were home with your wife and kids."

I hesitated. "Well, yeah, but things are different now."

She raised concerned eyebrows. "How?"

"Sarge, didn't you hear about Specialist Mitch Mosely?"

"No. Who's he?"

"A buddy. He was from near my hometown. His wife and mine were close friends. And he had twin boys."

I felt my blood pressure rise. "During the first day of the ground war, he drove his field ambulance over a land mine when we breached the Iraqi defensive line. He's dead."

"Sir, I'm real sorry to hear that, but . . ."

"But it should have never happened!" I seethed. "After we got to Saudi, I prayed every day that that all of us docs and medics would come home from the war safe. But Mitch was blown away." I tried to control my tears, but they poured out anyway. "And his wife is a widow. God didn't really care. Prayers didn't help at all."

The Humvee shook violently as its worn tires hit a bomb crater. Vernardo shook her head and squinted through the smudged windshield. "Major Roth says that those water towers are on the north side." She leaned out the window. "There they are. Ahead to the left."

We turned onto a dirt road. Two immense steel tanks mounted on scaffolds loomed in the distance.

The Humvee approached stone huts in front of the towers. A crowd of Iraqi boys encircled us.

Vernardo stopped. Boys stretched scrawny arms and begged, "Food, food!"

She scrutinized the kids. "Let's find the village emir to get permission to collect some samples."

Vernardo reached into her helmet bag and pulled out a sack of hard candy and balloons. "These should keep 'em distracted." We climbed out. I slipped an ammo clip into my Colt .45.

As Vernardo passed out the candy and balloons, the boys surged forward. The sergeant conversed with them. A slender, bearded Iraqi man in Western-style clothes stepped out of the nearest hut and limped toward us. The man's hand came to rest on my uniform sleeve. I fought an urge to withdraw my arm.

He introduced himself. "My name is Jamael. Can you give me something for my wounded foot?"

I bent down and looked at his swollen right heel. It bore a nasty laceration surrounded by inflamed skin. "Sir, you have a wound that looks infected. You need antibiotics to treat that, but we don't have any with us."

I pulled out a field dressing from my first aid kit and handed it to him. "But this can help."

He pulled it open and wrapped his foot.

"Who is the emir here?" I asked. "We'd like to get permission to inspect those towers here and to test the water to see if it's okay."

"I am the emir. Of course, sirs. You can do what you must."

The man's graciousness and cordial demeanor made me uncomfortable.

"Thank you, Jamael. Come ride with us to the towers."

We pulled up to the tanks and found two black-robed Iraqi women squeezing a canvas hose on the ground that led to one of the towers. The hose had no water to spare. Two sandaled Iraqi men clad in gray robes stood in the background and silently glared.

Sergeant Vernardo and I climbed out to inspect the towers while Jamael watched from his seat. Square metal tanks stood on steel scaffolds ten feet off the ground. The tanks had no visible water source. They appeared to hold water transported in from somewhere else.

Vernardo finished the inspection and we returned to the Humvee. "Sir," she said, "that rusted pump motor hasn't worked in years. But if I can get a tool kit, I can fix it."

"Great, Sarge. Let's head back to base. You can borrow a kit from the motor pool and we can come back tomorrow. Then these people will have water to drink."

We climbed back into the Humvee. I turned to Jamael. "We'll be back here tomorrow to fix that pump. And I'll bring along some antibiotics from our field hospital to treat your foot."

The next afternoon, I passed out candy to our entourage of Iraqi kids, and Sergeant Vernardo managed to bring the ancient pump motor back to life. Water sputtered from the cracked canvas hose. She collected samples and packed them in our cooler.

Jamael joined us at the Humvee. Questioning eyes moved to my uniform. "Why do you Americans wear dark green uniforms? Do you know that Iraqi soldiers wear such clothes?"

"I'm sorry, but these are the uniforms the American Army has given us. We'll be on our way. And we'll get back to you about the test results. Your people do need water."

"Americans killed my brother."

I fought to maintain composure. "When? How?"

"American bombers came over Baghdad one night. My brother, his wife and childrens, and many others took shelter in a bunker underneath the city. A bunker buster bomb fell on them. Over two hundred forty persons died."

My knees weakened. I remembered reading a *Stars and Stripes* article describing bombing sorties during the Desert Storm air war. American military intelligence had erred in targeting a civilian bomb shelter as an Iraqi military intelligence headquarters. The bunker suffered a direct hit. Scores of innocent Iraqi men, women, and children died.

"Jamael, I . . . I'm sorry."

He looked at the ground.

I reached into my pocket and pulled out a plastic bottle of antibiotic pills. "Here, I picked these up for you. This should treat that foot infection."

He took the bottle and nodded. "Thank you, Doctor. I will pray for you."

I stammered. "What? Why?"

He beamed. "I'm not only the village emir, but also the imam. I am, what you say in American, a pastor. I lead my Shiite persons in prayers at the Safwan mosque. My wife and four childrens live in a hut near the village marketplace."

"I would like to visit your mosque, Jamael."

His smile faded. "The mosque is heavily damaged. American artilleries and bombs destroyed the roof and one wall." He looked into my eyes. "But I forgive you and your military, Doctor Hanson. I hope that American and Iraqi people can be friends."

He thought for a moment. "Doctor Hanson, it is soon time for afternoon prayers. I have to go. I and my people will pray for you and your family."

Goosebumps formed on my neck.

Straight white teeth showed from behind thin lips as he grinned. "Doctor, it says in the Holy Qur'an of the Book of Ha Mim, 'Those who believe and do good, for them is a reward never to be cut off.'"

"Thank you, Jamael."

"Doctor Hanson, I hope to meet you again, when we have peace and no more war."

I rested my right hand on Jamael's shoulder. He put his arm around my shoulder. "Thank you, Doctor, for helping my village people." His countenance glowed. Tears streamed down my cheeks. I hugged him.

Back at base that night, I stood outside the tent studying the shimmering stars. I had provided physical healing to Jamael, and he had brought enormous spiritual healing to me. The violent death of my close friend had filled my heart with bitterness and anger. I had had no time for prayer or worship. But my meeting with Jamael forever changed my attitude about "those who believe."

Iraqi civilians suffered tremendously from the war, especially Jamael. He forgave me and offered his unconditional friendship though his brother died from American ordnance.

The realization hit me as forcefully as an exploding cluster bomb. God forgives *all* sinners, including me. Jesus Christ was my Savior, and he died not only for my sins but also for those of Jamael and his congregation.

Peace and forgiveness replaced bitter anger in my soul. My friend's death had put a barrier between me and my God. But that meeting with Jamael brought me nearer than ever to Jesus. I looked forward to offering a prayer back home for him and his worshipers.

~ *Clement Hanson*

Daddy's Girl

"I'M GOING TO have a good time, and no woman and two little kids are going to keep me from it," my father announced as he slammed the door behind himself.

At least he had gone without beating my mother this time. This conflict had started when Dad had asked Mother to press his clothes. Since it was only a few days before Christmas, and we had no presents or trees, I thought maybe he was going out to buy something for us.

As Mom pressed the pants, she found a receipt for a watch from a local jeweler. When she questioned Dad, he calmly reported that he'd bought the watch for another woman he'd fallen in love with.

Mom began to cry. Though I was only six, I was stunned. And my little sister Wanda crawled off to shelter—as she often did when the beatings started.

To prevent a blowup, Mom pressed the suit without further comment, and Dad strode out the door to his other woman.

A few days later, he returned without an explanation, and Mom welcomed him back with no questions. The abuse started again. Dad often erupted into violent rages, taking his anger out on Mom and my sister, Wanda. For some reason he was usually tender and kind to me. I was "Daddy's little girl," and I loved him with all my heart, but I still faced nightmares and the day-time terror that he would one day kill my mother.

I now realize that my mother was the typical battered woman. She defended my father, taking the blame for the beatings he gave her. "If I could only be a better wife," she often said, "he wouldn't lose his temper."

But even at my young age, I knew better. Mom was a gentle woman who trusted the promises of Psalm 27:13: "I had fainted, unless I had believed to see the goodness of the Lord in the land of the living."

When I questioned her faith in a heavenly Father who didn't seem to care, Mother would quote the next verse of the psalm: "Wait on the Lord: be of good courage, and he shall strengthen thine heart: wait, I say, on the Lord."

I had no one to talk to about my trauma-filled life, because Dad pretended to be a model Christian to others. At the small mission we attended, Dad was respected as one of the most spiritual members. Realizing that I could tell no one about what was going on in our home, I slipped into a deep depression. I became withdrawn and morose. Little Wanda lived in fear. Yet Mother was blind to the damage my father was doing to her two little girls, physically, emotionally, and spiritually.

My father finally left our family for good. We were destitute, but once people got over their shock at Dad's actions, they rallied behind us. Still, there were many times we went to bed hungry, and often Mom was ill. Her faith never wavered, but my heart grew colder. Though the pastor visited us often, he could not answer my question: How could a loving heavenly Father stand by (idly, I thought) and let a family sink into poverty and despair, as ours had done? How could I trust God when he'd allowed our family to suffer so much at the hands of my father?

Mom did not want to work outside our home, so she bought an old Maytag washer and became the neighborhood washer woman, working out of the rundown house we rented. I was seven years old and Wanda was four when we began picking up laundry from neighbors for Mom to wash and iron. One of the few pleasant memories I have from those days is sitting on the floor beneath Mom's ironing board, playing jacks while she ironed clothes around me. Mother was diligent and hardworking, so her business grew to capacity. But she was often ill, and we still needed help.

When we heard that Dad had a good job, Mother went to court to force him to pay child support. As the court process dragged out, hatred grew in my soul toward my father, his live-in girlfriend, and her four children. I wondered if the day would ever come when our family would be delivered out of our misery and pain, as Psalm 27:13 seemed to promise. I placed the blame for the hopelessness of my life not only on my earthly father's shoulders, but also on my Heavenly Father. I was angry with them both for deserting me. Through it all, Mom never lost her faith that the Lord would see us safely through. Each evening she knelt at her bedside and cried as she begged God to bring her husband back home. Nearby, and with tears of my own soaking my pillow, I drifted off to sleep begging God to keep him away.

When I was nine years old, the Ringling Brothers Circus came to town. Unexpectedly, Dad asked Mom if he could take me. Wanda was too young, he explained, to take along.

"I'll have her home before dark," he promised. Mom was reluctant, but I'd never seen a circus, so I begged to go. She gave in.

"I'm going to pick up some other kids to go with us," Dad announced as he pulled up in front of an apartment building about three miles from our house. When we entered a first-floor apartment, Dad reached up and pushed the chain lock across the door behind us. Panic set in and I screamed, "Let me out of here!"

He shoved me into a chair and told me to shut up.

A dark-haired woman appeared who tried to calm me down. "It will be all right," she kept saying. Dad explained that he was leaving with his new family for Texas, and that I was going with them. "There is no reciprocity between Texas and West Virginia, which means your mother can't have me jailed for nonsupport there. She can if I stay here. You're my favorite, and I'm taking you with me."

Terrified, I jumped out of the chair and tried to reach the lock on the door, but I couldn't. Turning around, I saw a young towheaded boy peeping around the corner at me. Picking up a lamp, I screamed that if they didn't let me out of there I'd throw it through the window.

Dad and his girlfriend didn't know what to do with an out-of-control child, so without another word he went to the door and pulled back the lock.

I ran all the way from that apartment building to my house. Scared that my father would follow me in his car, I kept to the hills, away from the roads. For the first time in my life I begged God, with whom I was not on speaking terms, for His divine help.

When I arrived home hysterical and gasping for breath, Mother took all the blame for my agony. "I shouldn't have taken him to court," she said. We hugged each other and cried.

Yet, in spite of the fact that God had answered my prayers and saved me from my father, my lack of trust for His protection continued to haunt me.

One Sunday when I was fourteen, our pastor delivered a sermon sent straight from the Lord Jesus Christ to me. Using John Chapter 10 as a springboard, the pastor talked about growing up on a sheep farm and how his own father had cared for the family's sheep, making sure they were safely within the sheepfold each night. He talked about the Lord Jesus Christ as the Good Shepherd who tenderly cared for His sheep, and that anyone who wanted could become one of His flock.

I took to heart everything the pastor said about Jesus and His love for me, but I wondered about the Heavenly Father. Could I really trust Him, too? Led by the Holy Spirit, my pastor spoke to that desperate need of mine as well. "Jesus Christ and the Father are one and the same," he said, "When you have seen Jesus, you've seen the Father, and everything that is true about the faithfulness of Christ is true of the Father, as well." My cold heart began to warm to my pastor's words.

The contrast between my earthly father and the heavenly One my pastor so clearly presented took hold. Everything my earthly father lacked, the Heavenly Father provided. He would never leave or forsake me. He would hold me securely and safely in His hands forever. Hearing of a loving God, who sent His Son to die for my sins that I might live forever, awakened my thirsty soul.

When the pastor read Matthew 19:14, "Suffer little children, and forbid them not, to come unto me: for of such is the kingdom of heaven," I knew it was my Savior's call to me. As soon as the closing hymn began, I ran forward to offer my young rebellious heart to the Lord Jesus Christ for cleansing. I, who had not felt the warmth of a father's hug for many years, spiritually curled up in my newfound Father's lap with His arms wrapped around me.

I was Daddy's little girl again.

~ Evelyn Rhodes Smith

Back from the Wild Side

SOMEWHERE INSIDE, MY brain knew it was cold. I saw white puffs when I breathed. I heard the wind whipping the chains on the courthouse flagpole. But as I put my head against the frosty green Pinto, I didn't feel cold. It was a good thing—I didn't know where my coat was.

If I had noticed the cold, I probably would also have noticed the stink. My shirt was soaked with a regurgitated mixture of grain alcohol and orange juice.

"What will we do with him this time?" I heard one of my cousins say.

"Doanworryboume," I slurred. Then everything went black as I felt my head bounce against the door. I came to later when I heard the word *hospital*. "Can't take him there," Ronnie said. "We'll all get in trouble."

"What if we can't bring him around the next time he goes out?" Phil argued. "Let's go to the emergency room."

"Mom and Dad will kill us if they find out we've been with Rick again," Danny said.

I tried to tell them I was fine. But the effort was too much. I was out again.

Being at my cousins' mercy was nothing new. I'd started drinking at sixteen, three years earlier, when my manager at

Dairy Queen had brought some whiskey to work. We started partying after closing every night. At first, he picked up the stuff for my coworkers and me because we were all underage. Later, we drove the twenty miles to the state line and found places that would sell to us.

I soon learned how to mix drinks for the quickest buzz. That was my purpose: to get drunk as rapidly as possible. Once drunk, I felt free. I could be as goofy as I liked—do things that I would never do while sober. I felt free from the lonely outsider I'd been ever since moving from Los Angeles. And I felt free from the guilt of knowing I was the biggest hypocrite around.

I knew that what I was doing was not right. I'd been raised in a Christian home and had accepted Christ as my Savior while still a young child. In my old Los Angeles church of 500, I was pegged as a leader. People thought I might grow up to be an evangelist.

But when I was thirteen, we had moved to Missouri. Our tiny new country church offered no spiritual challenge. We didn't have any activities or a youth group. I wasn't a leader anymore. Without that motivation, my Bible reading became sketchy. And because I'd been considered a super Christian, I saw myself as above the law, figured I didn't have to worry about toeing any marks or following the rules. I didn't consider a lot of things I did as sin because I thought I was too good to sin.

So when my manager introduced me to alcohol, it didn't seem like a major step away from God. After all, it was just a little bit of stuff to drink—it wasn't like it would change who I was, or that I'd become a drunkard.

I was still going to church every week. I felt the Holy Spirit's conviction sometimes, but I ignored it. Soon I became callous. My parents didn't have a clue about my drinking—they were more worried about drugs, which weren't even an issue for me. They caught me coming home drunk a time or two but were too naïve to realize it.

My cousins all knew, though—they were the ones I usually drank with. My Aunt Fernie and Uncle Buck had recently found out, too. They didn't tell my parents, but they had forbidden my cousins to spend time with me. Once I'd been the spiritual leader of my family. Now I was the black sheep, the bad influence, the outcast.

When I came to again, I tried to focus on the car's dome light. I could hear steps shuffling through the gravel.

"Donny said we can't take Rick into his house," Danny said. "He doesn't want to see Rick in that shape. He said he's sick of it."

"Aren't we all," Phil muttered.

Even as drunk as I was, I felt fury rising in me. Of all my cousins, I'd been closest to Donny. And now, he didn't want to see me? Wasn't there for me when I needed him?

"Take me home," I demanded groggily, focusing on Phil's face in the seat beside me.

"Yeah, I think he'll make it now," Phil said. The dome light went off.

At the same time, a light went on in my brain. I realized I was tired. Tired of living just to party. I was tired of the expense; that's why I'd started mixing grain alcohol and fruit juice—it was cheaper. I was tired of feeling like I didn't belong. That's why I'd started drinking. In the quest to gain friendship and acceptance, I was losing the people who meant the most to me.

Most of all, I was sick of being a hypocrite.

After that night, I kept drinking, but it stopped being fun. A few weeks later, on New Year's Eve, I walked into a party. Instead of celebration, I saw the emptiness in my friends' eyes. I knew there was a better life waiting for me. And I knew the first step to getting there was going across town, where my church was holding a watch night service.

When the pastor gave an invitation, I nearly ran to the altar. This time my commitment was a lifelong dedication. I was tired of what I'd done and wanted to put the old life behind me forever.

Immediately, the drinking stopped. Even though I already knew the Bible pretty well, I was like a new Christian. Hungry to learn, I spent hours reading my Bible and praying. The pastor got me involved in leadership again and frequently checked on me, encouraging me to keep growing spiritually.

I couldn't help telling others about my faith. After doing the partying scene, I knew it didn't really bring the fun or fulfillment it promised. When I walked back into a relationship with Christ, I embarked on the best lifestyle a person could live. I wanted everybody else to live that lifestyle, too.

More than twenty-five years later, I still feel that way. I'm partly glad for my prodigal experience. Some Christians are wishy-washy because they're curious about what it would be like to walk on the wild side. I've been there. I know it's destructive, not fulfilling. As a result, it's easier for me to maintain a lifelong commitment. And as my own kids have hit the ages where they start to wonder about the drinking that so many of their friends get busted for, I've been able to tell them, "Look, it's not worth it. I know. I've been there. You don't want to detour your faith." Fortunately, so far God's used my experiences to help my kids be friends with others who don't know Jesus—without my kids getting sucked into the lifestyle. And I've been able to talk to my sons' friends about it, too.

I've found that there's too much benefit to having a clean relationship with Jesus, and not depending on anything else to fill the voids in my life. I'm glad I came back to Him . . . I'll never walk away again.

~ *Rick Stock, as told to Jeanette Gardner Littleton*

Seeking Security

"YOU DON'T NEED to go forward—you're already a Christian!" Donna hissed at me.

Throughout the football stadium, people walked down to the field to talk and pray with volunteers who were called counselors. The speaker's message had touched me, and I wanted to be down praying with one of those leaders. But I stayed in my seat, so confused about how to know God.

All my life I had I heard about God. Raised in a very devout Catholic family, I took religion seriously and attended mass as often as I could. My parents had taught and modeled the importance of believing in God. Stories of saints and martyrs inspired me. I longed to match their spirituality and tried to follow their godly example, even though I often failed. Catechism and homilies didn't quite fill my quest to know God better, either.

Every day I recited prayers I learned in childhood, hoping they were reaching God. At times I even refused pleasures and endured discomfort, hoping these little earthly sacrifices might make God happy. I tried to serve Him, but I wondered how I could ever be good enough for him.

I also looked for a relationship with God in the parochial school I attended. I admired the nuns and planned to join the convent when I grew up. Then I figured I could totally dedicate my life to Christ. When I transferred to a public high school, however, I changed my mind.

I longed for a boyfriend, but no guys ever asked me out. On the contrary, I was a natural target for teasing since I was tall and skinny, with a face full of acne. Cruel words brought tears to my eyes while my tormenters laughed. I felt as if no one liked me and began to doubt if God did—or if He was even real. If He existed and cared, I reasoned, why didn't He do something to relieve my misery?

During these years, I had some Christian friends, but no one ever explained to me how to be "saved." Sometimes people asked if I was a Christian. I answered yes. But when others said something about being saved, I did not grasp what they meant. How could anyone know for sure that he or she would make it to heaven? I greatly feared the alternative—unending torment in hell.

During my senior year in high school, I began to experience bouts of depression. Life seemed worthless, and I became obsessed with death. Facing it terrified me, but part of me longed for such an escape. I became so miserable I even considered taking my own life. My mother took me to the doctor, but he didn't offer any real help. I tried to snap out of it on my own, escaping into the busyness of school and activities.

That's when my locker partner, Donna, took me to that crusade held at the local football stadium. After that night, I kept up my quest of trying to figure out what it meant to be saved. The next fall, after I graduated from high school, a friend encouraged me to watch a Billy Graham crusade on television. *Maybe this will help me understand the whole matter of salvation*, I thought.

My dad was watching sports in the living room, so I went out to the old television in the family room. Dad called after me, "I don't know why you want to watch that, but I guess it won't hurt you." I knew he didn't approve, but I was so spiritually hungry I just had to see what this religious leader had to say.

I drank in every word. The song lyrics, the message—everything spoke to me personally. As if a spotlight illumined my mind, understanding dawned. I realized that although I'd tried to be good enough for God all of my life, I'd missed the vital step. I was trying to win God's approval without really knowing who He was. All of the various pieces I'd been taught came together. I realized I could only come to God by starting a relationship with His Son, Jesus Christ. Though I'd tried to be good, I knew I'd still committed sins. I realized that Jesus had, in some spiritual way, taken on my sins when He died on the cross so many years ago. When Billy Graham invited people to join him in a prayer of repentance—of admitting sins and asking forgiveness for the sins—I eagerly responded. I turned my life over to Jesus.

Finally I understood what people meant when they spoke of a personal relationship with God. Although I had talked to God all my life, it had been like relating to someone at a distance. Now He dwelt within me. I truly *knew* Jesus as my personal Savior. My doubts and fears had disappeared, and I could hardly contain the joy and excitement inside me.

My feelings of not being loved simply disappeared. In fact, I started feeling such an overwhelming love for others that I almost had to bite my tongue to keep from telling everyone I met, "I love you." I even felt a strong love for my younger brother and sister, whom I had merely tolerated. My entire life was transformed.

How wonderful to be able to talk with God about anything, instead of repeating rote, traditional prayers! I began reading God's Word. What I had done before out of dry duty now became a blessing. The Bible seemed so fresh and new and alive. I memorized Psalm 23 and other Scriptures I found special. Discovering spiritual truths was like finding buried treasure. It was all so exciting that I started to tell others how I now really knew God!

Since that day I gave my life to the Lord, I no longer fear rejection or dread hell. I know for certain God has a home prepared for me in Heaven. I long to meet Him face to face and to spend eternity in His presence. Without Him, I don't know where I would be today. With Him in my life, I am secure, and so is my future.

∼ Mary A. Hake

What My Students Taught Me

I GRABBED MY keys and hurried to the school parking lot. Although little mountains of dirty snowed still ringed the lot, a certain warmth in the usually chilly Michigan air reminded me that spring break was only a few days away. I had just finished an after-school session with two students, Joe and Amy. Both new Christians, they were excited to share their newfound "joy" with me. I found the experience more disconcerting than comforting.

"How dare they?" I thought as I began my drive home. I was a Sunday school teacher who had gone to church all my life. Certainly, I knew the Bible better than two high school students who were average at best on their ACT scores. I had served on numerous committees, planned vacation Bible schools, and purchased Sunday school material by the truckload. But I had heard something in their voices, an enthusiasm I knew I lacked. Determinedly, I chalked that up to youth.

As I pulled into my driveway, the memory of their excitement continued to eat at me. What did they have that seemed so attractive to me? So elusive? It had to do with peace, which seemed to come from a personal relationship with God, a relationship as carefree and close as they had with their friends. How was that possible at such a young age? *Ridiculous,* I thought as I began making dinner.

My life was perfect. As a part-time guidance counselor, I had the best of both worlds. I could be an all-around mother, like my mom had been, but I also had a career that I loved and was good at. My husband was wonderful and loving and a great father besides. Our income had allowed us some nice "toys" of neighborhood envy but not enough to spoil our children. So why did I have this feeling that I was missing something?

Over the weekend, the idea of a personal relationship with Jesus Christ began to unravel me. I searched out my Bible and flipped through the pages—not really a daily experience for me, but more like a lifeline in times of crisis. The stories were all there: Abraham, Moses, Daniel, David and Goliath, Ruth. I had recited them many times, but now my heart began to see them as my eyes never had.

Let's not take this Christian thing too seriously, I thought. People might think I'd turned into one of those Jesus freaks. Just be good enough to get into that elusive heavenly home but down to earth enough to be human after all.

Then a verse in Revelation, Revelation 3:16, jumped out at me. The scripture explained that if a person is not hot or cold, but lukewarm, God will spit us out of his mouth. *Lukewarm . . . that was me.* I was the Queen of Lukewarm.

Now I faced a decision. If my remaining lukewarm did not please God, then I had to make a choice. The fence-riding days of carefully walking the middle road, without being a whole-hearted Christian, were over. The thought wouldn't leave my mind.

The next day happened to be Good Friday. I remember announcing to my husband, "I think we should go to the Good Friday service."

He looked at me strangely as this had not been a practice in our home, but he agreed to go. We let our son and daughter stay home as we made the short trek to the familiar building that held four generations of my family's history. Everything was there, all the pomp and circumstance, but nothing was personal about it.

We attended the service, and I expected the miracle to happen then. I wanted the joy and peace that Amy and Joe had shared. Instead I felt nothing, empty, miserable. Why was it escaping me? When we returned to our car, I fought the tears that were in my eyes. My husband glanced at me and said, "Honey, what's wrong?"

I couldn't answer at first but finally choked out that I needed to return to church. He swung around the block and pulled into a parking place. I jumped out of the car, mumbling that I'd be just a minute.

I hurried into the empty sanctuary. No one was there—what would I have said if someone had been? I sat in a pew and realized that this was my fence-jumping moment. To this day I can't remember my words. All I remember is the peace that flooded over me as I decided to live wholeheartedly for Christ and asked Him to fill my whole life. I felt every fiber of my being change, leaving me at complete rest. I don't know how long I sat there, but I slipped out without anyone noticing . . . except Jesus, whose image looked down at me from the wooden cross at the front of the sanctuary. He was there—not up on the cross, but His Holy Spirit shared my pew.

The change came about gradually, not like the strike of lightning I had imagined. I grew in my faith and finally discovered that personal relationship my two students had witnessed to me, now many years before. I always said that my best teaching experiences came when students taught me and not the other way around. Jesus knew that. I went on to form a Bible study at my high school, and I began each year with this verse: "Let no man despise thy youth; but be thou an example of the believers, in word, in conversation, in charity, in spirit, in faith, in purity." (1 Timothy 4:12) That's what some young people did for me.

～ Debbie Bentley

How I Found True Love

I ENTERED OUR bedroom carrying my favorite edition of
Grimms' fairy tales. Curled under the covers was my husband
of four months. My heart swelled with love until I saw what he
had chosen for his bedtime reading.

"Not the Bible!" I shouted. "Only geeks read the Bible."

"It's helping," he replied. I knew he'd been picking it up
since his grandfather's funeral. Instead of understanding, I
threw my book at him. "Read that!" I screamed. "It has a lot
more truth than what you're holding!"

My temper often flared up unreasonably concerning God.
My parents raised me to go to church. Unfortunately, though
they required attendance, my endless questions met with
"Because" or "You'll understand when you're older." Though I
learned Bible stories and heard that God was love, I couldn't see
it. Religion seemed all rules without answers, and God seemed
its cruel taskmaster.

Like most kids I knew, I went to confirmation classes
when I reached middle school. As I attended, my unanswered
questions and increasing doubts about God grew. A couple of
months before my confirmation day, my grandmother died. My
grief flamed disbelief into hatred. How could He take her from
me when I had prayed for her healing? I wanted nothing more

of this capricious God. I studied the occult. I started smoking and joined a rough crowd.

"I will not be confirmed," I told my mother. "I don't believe in it."

"You finished the classes. You will be confirmed."

I was present at the ceremony. But I inserted a "not" within each statement of faith.

For the next two years, a voice I'd encountered during a séance gave me visions of the future. I read palms. I planned astrological charts. I felt powerful and liked the attention. Then, as an exchange student in France, my host family took me to a cult worship service. I don't know what group it was, but it terrified me. People dressed in black went into a room to meet with their leader. Then they came out looking drugged or possessed. So I repeated the only prayer I remembered from all my years at church, the Lord's Prayer. I left the occult that day.

To fully break from the occult, I tried God. I was rebaptized and taught summer Bible school. But in my high school classes I studied existentialism. According to existentialism, my choices and thoughts created my identity. I chose my answers. That made more sense than an unresponsive God and people who wouldn't talk about Him. I went to church Sundays and attended youth group on Saturdays. But Monday through Friday, I believed the gospel according to French existentialist Jean Paul Sartre.

So when Gary married me, though I called myself a Christian, I was an existentialist with a hatred of God from way back.

The first month of our marriage passed without any arguments about religion. In northern Michigan, there weren't a lot of options on Sunday. I tried the local version of my denomination, but I didn't like the pastor. As there were no nearby Baptist churches, Gary didn't even bother. We stayed in and read the paper.

Then Gary's grandfather died. Pappa—a deacon, lay pastor, and Bible teacher—had been Gary's spiritual mentor. Gary felt his loss deeply. So Gary did as Pappa taught him. Gary read his Bible. Gary turned to Jesus.

Recommitted, Gary started praying for me. That was infuriating. I told him time and time again that if I wanted his prayers, I would have requested them.

If I had been willing to delve into my soul, I could have admitted that I needed prayer. Everything I earned from my four part-time jobs paid for graduate school. Gary's airman salary barely covered our expenses. I squeezed studying and classes into my packed schedule. I was gaining weight. The stomach pains that I'd had since high school no longer went away with medicine. And I was lying to Gary every night when I got home from work and he sniffed at the air. I swore that I'd quit smoking, and that all he smelled was the restaurant's atmosphere, but that wasn't true. I was a wreck.

Then I became a waitress at the local country club. My Christian boss, John, was a large man with a voice deeper than nearby Lake Huron. And when this former biker told the waitresses that we couldn't leave work until he prayed, I complied.

As I got to know John, I argued with him about the Bible. He was unflappable. "I know it's true," he insisted. "Jesus changed me. Or as it says in 2 Corinthians 5:17, 'If any [one] be in Christ, he is a new creature: old things are passed away; behold, all things are become new.'" In response, I called my boss a doddering fool. He would always smile. "I'm glad I'm a fool for Christ!"

After I'd been working with him and arguing with him for three months, he gave me a challenge. "You've got some extra time over the winter break from school. So consider this my assignment to you. You say the Bible's full of error. Prove it. Read the book of John."

I knew my education could prove John wrong. But as I read an entire book of the Bible—instead of Bible stories and books about the Bible—something changed. It began to get interesting. Not to get Gary's hopes up, I read when he was at work or out fishing. In the quiet of the house and a northern winter, I learned why the Bible existed. "But these are written that ye might believe that Jesus is the Christ, the Son of God; and that by believing ye might have life in his name" (John 20:31).

Life sounded like a wonderful and impossible gift. Though only in my twenties, I coughed a lot. My puffy body no longer felt like my own or moved as easily. My stomach would unexpectedly blow up like a balloon in excruciating pain. In other words, I felt dead. But Jesus offered life.

When I finished the book of John, I went to the beginning of the Gospels and read on. In Matthew 5:48, the Bible said to get to heaven I had to be perfect just as God is perfect. Perfect? I couldn't even be good on a regular basis. My efforts couldn't get me to heaven. The occult had made hell and death real to me. I didn't want either of those to be my final destination. The Bible said the answer was faith in Jesus. He alone paid for my sins on the cross. "I am the way, the truth and the life: no man cometh unto the Father, but by me" (John 14:6).

Alone on my twenty-third birthday, I had had enough of trying to work through all my issues and myself on my own. "Help me, Jesus," I prayed. "Take over my life."

To my absolute amazement, God did want my life and answered my prayers. Jesus started changing me. My stomach problem went away immediately. I prayed with a pastor to quit smoking and though the temptation persisted, never picked up a cigarette again. My tempestuous anger dimmed—overwhelmed by God's love.

Gary and I began meeting with other families in a home church. One Saturday afternoon as we held hands to worship, Gary whispered, "I love you." Our union in Christ began that day.

Has life been perfect since that moment? No. That only happens in the fairy tales I used to read. But I do know that our united faith has kept us together for twenty-three years now through the birth of two boys, a variety of homes and careers, and problems and trials of all shapes and sizes. Because we both know, that though we love each other, our true love is found in Jesus.

~ *Susan A. J. Lyttek*

Return to My Father

I WANTED NOTHING to do with God or church or anything spiritual. My dad had served as a pastor to several struggling congregations during my growing-up years, and I had seen enough backbiting and complaining in the so-called body of Christ to forever turn me off to organized religion.

Dad finally became so frustrated he left the ministry. A few years later, when I was just nineteen, he died from a blood clot. I had begged God to heal him, even offering my life in exchange for his. Since God had not answered my prayer, I completely turned my back on Him. If He ignored me, I could certainly forget Him. I quit going to church and stopped praying—not that it had ever done me much good anyway.

After that, I made my own way, working hard and finding fun wherever I could. As the oldest child, I supported my family while Mom went back to college. Then she remarried, and I was freed from that financial responsibility. At age twenty-two, I had my life all to myself, and I intended to enjoy my independence. Hunting, fishing, and camping with my dog made life worth living.

My selfish plans changed course when I met a dark-haired eighteen-year-old named Mary. We quickly fell in love, and six months later we married. Mary was a new Christian, and she tried to share her faith with me. I not only resisted her efforts but also criticized her spiritual life. I forbade her to sic the pastor on me—I hated it when hypocrites tried to shove Jesus down my throat.

Mary tried not to be too pushy, but she could not keep quiet about something so vital to her. I didn't mind if she got religious, as long as she didn't bug me to join in. She often listened to Christian programs and filled our home with Christian music and literature. Our young daughters followed her lead. They loved to sing "Jesus Loves Me" and to play church or listen to Bible stories. Often they asked, "Why doesn't Daddy go to church with us?" Yet I stubbornly resisted.

Then my wife of almost seven years began suffering intense pain from cysts in her ovaries. Her medicine no longer brought much relief. This agony nearly incapacitated her. Besides her physical trauma, she felt overwhelmed with guilt for neglecting the house and the children. I pitched in as much as I could, but I hated to see her suffer so.

I knew Mary and her friends had been praying for her healing. But, just like my experience with my dad, they had received no positive answer. The situation seemed hopeless. *Mary is only twenty-five. Will we face this the rest of our lives?* I wondered. *Life sure hasn't turned out like I'd envisioned.*

Unable to stand the tension at home, I often escaped to a piece of property we owned about twelve miles from town. Although I told Mary I went there to do some work, I sometimes just sat in the peaceful pasture, relaxing and thinking about life. My mind groped for solutions, for hope. I felt so helpless.

Even though I mocked Mary's faith, I secretly admired her perseverance. She refused to give up on God. In fact, she said she knew she couldn't make it through a single day without Him.

Maybe there really is something to this after all, I reflected. Stubbornly I shook my head. Resisting God's tug on my heart, I squelched the quiet voice calling me back.

When Mary couldn't bear the pain any longer, she scheduled an appointment with a surgeon to discuss a hysterectomy. Although the nurse told Mary she was too young to consider such surgery, the doctor agreed that it was the logical course of action. They set the operation for June 23, the day my two-week vacation began. What a way to spend our seventh anniversary!

We arranged for our daughters to stay with their great-grandparents until Mary could care for them again. The girls looked forward to the fun they would have at Grandma and Granddad's, oblivious to the serious situation their mommy faced.

As I waited during Mary's surgery, I wondered if everything would turn out okay. Will life get back to normal? What if something happens? The surgeon said there was always the possibility of a stroke or even death . . . no, nothing can go wrong.

Relief washed over me when the doctor told me that all had gone well. He said Mary should recover quickly and be fine.

Unfortunately, this wasn't the case. Mary developed an infection. Her fever matched the growing heat of summer. Weeks of limited activity and extreme pain sapped her strength, and she had no reserves to draw from. It seemed she had traded one form of suffering for another.

"It's not that bad," Mary said. "This doesn't compare to the pain I had before." But she grew more depressed as her days of confinement dragged on.

Tests showed Mary's blood count was too low, so the doctor ordered a blood transfusion. Mary tried to call me at home with this news, but I was gone. Her pastor was out of town and her parents away, so she could not reach anyone for comfort. Mary panicked and thought she must be dying if such drastic means were being taken. When Mary finally caught me at home, I hurried to the hospital. The chaplain had visited and prayed with Mary, trying to calm her. I sat by my wife's bed and held her hand, still feeling powerless. She was too young to die. I didn't want to lose her. In my desperation, I turned to God. I suddenly realized that I did believe in Him. Whether I always had deep inside or whether I was simply returning to the lost beliefs of my childhood, it didn't matter. Eleven years of barriers crumbled as I humbled myself before Him. I heard His gentle voice tenderly say, "I still love you, Ted. You can come back to me at any time."

"I love you too," I told Him. Amazingly, when I opened myself to Him, He was right there to help and comfort me. I felt like I had exchanged the weight of the world for a bright balloon. Still, I kept this transformation to myself as I continued to spend time with Mary at the hospital.

Ten days after her surgery, Mary was finally released. She was ordered to take walks to regain her strength and hasten her recovery. On one of our walks around the neighborhood, I said, "I think I'll start going to church with you." She almost fainted. Eventually I explained what had occurred between God and me.

Mary also shared a secret: "I felt like the Lord told me if I would go through with the surgery, He would use it to reach you."

I had to acknowledge He had done just that. Not only did I develop a personal relationship with the Lord, but Mary and I also grew closer. Now we no longer clash spiritually, but are united. With God in charge, we can face the future unafraid.

～ *Ted Hake, as told to Mary A. Hake*

He Knew Me

MY EARLIEST CHILDHOOD memories are of living in my grandparents' home, where there was love, laughter, security, and happiness. As a five-year-old child, my life was good.

When I was six, my mom married a man I'll call Tom. We left my grandparents' home and my life became a living nightmare. I was surrounded by drugs, alcohol, and abuse, both physical and mental. I watched my mom get beat up daily. I was hit or something was thrown at me more times than I care to remember. The sexual abuse was the worst, and it influenced my actions in years to come.

I hated my life. I was scared all the time and never knew what was going to happen when my stepdad got home from work. I lived in a nightmare that continued for five years.

I knew nothing of God.

But He knew me and had great plans for my life.

My five-year nightmare finally came to an end when my older sister attempted suicide. Child protective services got involved. We were removed from the home and placed in the temporary custody of an aunt until my mom could get clean and find us a place to live. My mom left Tom at that point because she wanted to be with us. Life seemed to be getting better, but it only lasted a little while. The next two years are a blur. All I recall is that as an eleven-year-old girl, I did whatever I wanted, whenever I wanted. There was no consistent or caring adult figure in my life. My mom, ironically enough, went back to Tom. I was not going back to that, so I stayed with different friends, carrying a bag of clothes from place to place. I tried to do the right thing. I tried to stay in school, but I got tired.

Then I got bad. I quit going to school—no one was around to make me go. I started living a destructive, unhealthy life. I welcomed the excitement of drugs and alcohol, and I was sexually promiscuous.

I knew nothing of God.

But He knew me. He created me, and He had great plans for my life.

Around my fourteenth birthday, my dad came into my life. He told me that he loved me, that he wanted me to come live with him. At first I thought it was a joke. I only vaguely remembered seeing him a couple of times. Why had he returned? What did he want of me? I figured I didn't need him—I was all grown up and could take care of myself. Besides, it was too late for him to try to be a father. I didn't realize then what a life preserver God had thrown me. I ended up grabbing it with both hands—never realizing how tightly I would have to hold on in the near future.

Less than a year after I moved to Hopkinsville, Kentucky, to live with this virtual stranger who was my father, I was diagnosed with Hodgkin's lymphoma. After numerous tests, my spleen was removed, and I started radiation therapy immediately. About the same time, I began my freshman year of high school.

I knew nothing of God.

But He knew me and had great plans for my life.

My first round of radiation therapy was successful, and I was pronounced in remission. So life became better than it had been since those long-ago years with my grandparents. I had a nice home to live in, food to eat, and I was never yelled at or hit. I began to be happy about life again.

I was even happier when I met a senior at my high school named Jason Merriss. Jason was a Christian. I began attending church with him and his family. I began to learn about someone named God and how much He loved me. I was interested but confused. If this God loved me so much, why had I spent eight years of my life in misery and so alone? But I kept going to church and I kept learning.

During my sophomore year in high school, I became very sick again. I couldn't stay awake and had night sweats, chills, and fevers. My cancer was back with a vengeance. I was so frightened. The second round of treatment was even worse than the first. I began chemotherapy. For three weeks in the hospital, I fought for my life.

Jason stood by me the entire time. All kinds of people I didn't even know came and prayed over me, sent me cards, and gave food to my family. Jason even shaved his head to match mine! I began to trust people again.

I knew *of* God but I still didn't know Him.

But God knew me. He loved me, and He healed me. I have now been in remission for over ten years.

So I began my junior year in high school with a clean bill of health and a boyfriend in college. By this time, Jason's relationship with God had been put on the back burner. Maybe I wasn't the best influence on this young Christian man, or maybe the temptation in our relationship was just too great. At any rate, in December of that year I got pregnant. My relationship with my dad had also become very strained, and telling him I was pregnant was one of the hardest things I ever had to do.

I was only seventeen. I had just had my last chemotherapy treatment, so there were many concerns about the baby being healthy and about my health as well. Jason and I were scared and uncertain about what to do. With the urging of people around us, we decided to get married. But no one would marry us because Jason was a Christian and I was not. For us to get married, I had to say something like, "Lord, I am a sinner. Please forgive me and come live in me. I give my life to you."

At that point I had no true understanding of how those words could change my life. So I simply said what they wanted me to say and did what they wanted me to do so I could get married.

Unfortunately, that was it. I didn't mean a single word I said, but I was married. Our healthy baby boy, Preston, was born the next August. The three of us began our new life together as a young family, never attending church, just living for ourselves.

Three years into our marriage, I began to fall apart. I decided I didn't want to be a mother or a wife anymore. I felt that I had missed out on life, and I decided to live the way I wanted. I returned to my destructive lifestyle, the drugs and alcohol that had been my downfall. Unfortunately, I was bringing my husband down with me. The familiar phrase "drive a man to drink" applied to us.

Finally, I moved out, and divorce knocked on the door. But our marriage was sacred to God. It wasn't over to Him, and He began to change our lives.

The turning point came one day when Jason arrived to pick up Preston. I hadn't seen Jason for a week. When he walked through the door, my heart seemed to stop beating. A glow surrounded my husband—a light, a presence hard to explain. Gone were the angry eyes, the hard face, the lines of hatefulness. Instead, I stared at a man completely at peace, with a gentleness on his face I had never seen before. It was amazing. Instead of departing with ugly, spiteful words, nothing was said at all. He had returned to the God of his youth, the God his parents had taught him to honor—the God that we had turned our backs on.

When Jason left, I began to cry. At that moment, so many things became clear to me. It was as though someone took off my blindfold, and now I could truly see everything. How destructive, selfish, careless, and hate-filled I was! I could see how lonely I was despite all the friends I had. For the first time in my life, I began to truly see Christ. When my eyes were opened that day, God began to heal me. He began to heal the broken person I was and then the broken marriage I had nearly destroyed.

I was beginning to know God, the God who knew me and had great plans for me.

My marriage was in serious trouble, but Christ can do anything, and He did. Doors began to open in awesome ways. Jason and I were able to move away from the people and things that were such a negative and destructive influence on us. We began attending church every week. I started to get to know my husband again. He was not the same person I'd met when I was fifteen or the young man I married at seventeen. He was now a man of God—a man who loved the Lord with all his being.

Six months after our reconciliation, I accepted Christ as my Lord and Savior. This time I meant it with all my heart and with all my soul. Jesus Christ changed my life from that point on. He has made me whole.

Finally, I know God. I am forgiven, and I have forgiven. I know He has great plans for me.

Jason and I have been married for ten years now. Our marriage is better than it has ever been. I love my husband more each day (well, most days!). He is my best friend and companion. Our children are not beaten or surrounded by drugs and alcohol. They have a safe place to live, a home of laughter and love. But most important, they are being raised on the foundation of Christ. My greatest desire is for all three of our children to grow up to love the Lord with all their hearts, all their souls, all their minds, and all their strength.

So did God have great plans for me? Absolutely! He is my joy, my love, my peace, my rock. Does He still have plans I know nothing about? Absolutely! Daily I live for Him, daily I strive to be more like His Son. I cannot wait to know Him even more and discover all the plans He has for me.

～ Shana L. Merriss

Convicted at a Concert

I HAD PURCHASED my ticket months ahead of time. So when I finally sat in the huge arena among the thousands of others waiting for the concert to begin, I tingled with anticipation. The woman next to me smiled at me and introduced herself, Judie, and her husband Marshall. They worked with a Christian organization on the University of Colorado campus in Boulder. I had gone to CU on a voice scholarship and sang in a band myself, but I had never heard of that group.

Our conversation flowed freely. Judie was friendly and confiding. She and Marshall kept telling me that their faith in God had made all the difference when life was difficult.

"Jo," Judie asked, "are *you* a Christian?"

That caught me off guard. *That's for church,* I thought, *not a rock concert.* At the same time, my brain automatically produced the requested data: taken to Christian church services as a child. It didn't matter that I doubted that God really cared about me, *if* He even existed. I smiled back and said confidently, "Yes, I'm a Christian."

But Judie persisted. "Do you know Jesus in a *personal* way?"

Jesus died a couple thousand years ago. How can anyone know Him personally? I thought. Confused, I asked, "How do you do that?"

Judie smiled and pulled a booklet out of her purse. I wondered how many booklets she carried with her.

"Jo, God loves you," she said, pulling my mind away from her purse.

Suuure, I thought. I stared at this couple and wondered, *If I'm a Christian, why don't I believe in God the way Judie and Marshall do?* Except for my grandmother, who talked about God like He was real, the Christianity I had experienced seemed hypocritical. That was why I had quit attending church years earlier, except an occasional Easter or Christmas.

I was relieved when the warm-up act took the stage, working the crowd with jokes. Now I didn't have to think about the enormity of what Judie had just read to me from her booklet—that Jesus had died for *me,* because no matter how hard I tried, I couldn't be good enough for God. And that in order to experience God's love, I needed to believe He had sent His Son, Jesus, to die in my place.

The long-awaited concert finally began, but the music didn't grab me as I'd expected it would. I couldn't totally block out the sparkle I saw in Judie and Marshall—I'd never seen that in *anyone* before. It seemed like the information they shared was waving a hand in my head to get attention.

After the concert, Marshall introduced me to their friends, who had been sitting all around me. We exchanged phone numbers and I left. Outside, enthusiastic men and women like Judie and Marshall weaved through the crowded sidewalks, handing out flyers about Jesus. I'd never encountered this kind of Jesus freak before.

The song "Jesus Loves Me" started playing in my head. I had learned it in Sunday school. We had even learned it in another language. But the Jesus I'd heard about did not care about me personally; He cared about everybody in the world. *Is someone trying to tell me something?* I wondered.

On the drive home I thought about my life. I had started partying in junior high. By the time I got to college, I commonly drank so much I didn't always know how I had gotten home. I was in and out of relationships, looking for some kind of meaning, some kind of love, some purpose for living. I had never really thought about it before, but on that drive home, I realized that I felt empty.

Home, I barely noticed my dog Jessie's playful *rrrrffff* for attention. I was curious about the booklet Judie had given me and couldn't wait to read it. For the first time in my life, I began to think that maybe going to church occasionally did not automatically make me a Christian. I'd always thought I was a good person—I didn't cheat on my income taxes; I returned change to clerks who gave me too much; I cared about my neighbors. But the booklet quoted a Bible verse that said that everyone had sinned and fallen short of God's glory (Romans 3:23). For the first time ever, I realized that something as small as a snotty remark I'd made earlier that day took me out of God's category of perfect.

I had always hated the word *sinner*. That night I realized I was one.

I knelt beside my bed—I didn't know why I knelt; it just seemed appropriate. I asked God to forgive me for my desire to live apart from Him, for my sin. I didn't see visions or hear bells, but I felt loved like never before. It was as if God was saying, "You are worth more than *anything* in the world to me." I couldn't comprehend a love that vast. I eagerly gave my life to Him, not knowing what that really meant, but hoping He would fill the emptiness inside me with His love and a purpose for living.

The booklet said that God had a plan for my life. What will God have in store for me now that I've become His child? I wondered.

The following day was full of promise, and I felt thankful for everything. I gave a short concert at a nursing home, and I found that I wanted to tell them about God. I wanted to tell them that I had a *personal* relationship with the Creator of the universe, and they could as well. *I'm turning into Judie!* I thought with surprise. My grandmother cried when I told her I'd become a Christian and hugged me fiercely. "Praise the Lord!" she'd said. "I've prayed for this for years." I started attending church and reading the Bible, as well as telling others how to know Jesus, and singing songs about the Lord. My life quickly filled with purpose.

A few years later I was diagnosed with multiple sclerosis, or MS, but I found that God still loved me and hadn't deserted me. As I studied the Bible, I learned that if God didn't choose to heal me miraculously, then He intended to use the MS in my life. As Romans 8:28 tells us, when we love God and serve him, all things work together for our good. Learning to live with the unpredictability of MS has daily tested my faith—I had to decide whether I'd turn to God in trust or turn from Him in rage because of encroaching disabilities. Early on, I decided to learn how to give thanks in all circumstances, as the Bible says (1 Thessalonians 5:18), and to reap all I can from the experience.

But that doesn't mean I give in to the disease. I've learned to ski, and my husband and I ride a tandem bike in MS150 bike tours. When the attacks immobilize me, I praise God because He *is* God—no matter what is happening—and He pours peace and joy into my heart. Nothing is more fulfilling and exciting than to know Christ intimately and to tell others about Him. I eagerly share His message during speaking engagements, but I also tell my neighbors, and I tell my friends. I tell my banker, my hairdresser, and my doctors—even the person seated next to me on an airplane!

And of course, I carry a stash of tiny booklets—just like the ones Judie shared with me the night of that concert.

~ *Jo Franz*

The God Who Knocks with Kindness

I REMEMBER IT was a beautiful day. "We won't be going to church today, honey," my mother told me. "Actually," she continued, "we probably won't go back to church again at all." I never knew what happened. My family had gone to church in our little West Virginia town every Sunday. Mommy and Daddy had been baptized in the river behind our house.

I was five at the time, and guess I was too little to remember God, for it seemed He left my life after that. Through the rough years of junior high and high school, I never knew Him. In four years of college, I never heard the faint knock of the Lord at my front door.

It was my third year in the magazine publishing industry, and boy, was I successful! "This year, Mel, we are actually going to double your salary." Hear God knocking? Obviously, I didn't need Him. I had a career, a husband whom I adored, and a beautiful baby girl. What a fabulous world I had created for myself. No one else could be responsible for all of this joy. I had dreams and goals, and they were coming true. I was in total control!

"Honey," my husband said to me on the way to the hospital for a very routine procedure. "I passed three funeral processions on the way to the hospital this morning. Do you think that could be a sign of things to come?"

"Don't be silly," I replied, "They've explained how simple this procedure is. No different than going to the dentist."

"We are just going to perform a minor surgery on your husband," the doctor told me. "In forty-five minutes he'll be out and in recovery. He can rest over the weekend and go back to work on Monday." I waited out those forty-five minutes with the other people whose family members were having procedures.

Time stretched on, and one by one the nurses came to call other people away. "Mr. Taylor, you may come see your wife now." "Mrs. Kelley, your nephew is in recovery, you may come see him now." The families that had begun the afternoon with me all left. By hour six, I was the only one remaining. No doctor came to see me. No reassuring nurse's voice informed me that my husband was safe in recovery.

As the seventh hour approached, the doctor himself came out to personally apologize for the wait.

"The surgery actually took a little longer than we planned. I wasn't able to finish and will have to keep your husband overnight. Please be assured, this kind of thing happens all the time. Your husband will be fine."

I was ecstatic that my husband was okay and that all the wild things going through my imagination had been wrong. My relief was so strong that it overpowered my ability to see how wrong this scenario was.

"Oh my goodness," I said when I woke up in my hospital cot the next morning and looked at my husband. Something was terribly wrong. He was puffed up like a Macy's Thanksgiving Day balloon. As it turned out, both his kidneys had shut down. How odd. His surgery had nothing to do with his kidneys at all.

Despite my husband's condition, the doctor finished his operation that day. We were now in the hospital indefinitely, as we had to wait and see how quickly we could start dialysis. At least things could not get any worse.

But things can *always* get worse. My husband's pancreas shut down, again for no apparent reason. Two days later, his lungs went. He was rushed to specialists at a hospital in Boston.

With my husband on life support, I began to get messages that people were praying for us. All over the country, people of every faith (and some with no known faith at all) were e-mailing and calling everyone they knew to pray for this poor man with a young wife and infant daughter. How could he be healed? The doctors hadn't a clue.

Even though the doctors advised me to go home and rest, I planted my feet firmly. For three weeks I was a permanent fixture at that hospital. One evening, I felt a rare call to leave his bedside. I went to the lobby and sat alone by the big window. A purple and orange sunset blanketed the Boston skyline, as if sent to give me peace when I had none. *Something that beautiful could only come from God,* I thought. I realized that I had been too busy taking care of everything in the hospital to even pray for my own husband. I looked up. "God, if you save him, I will love him even more than I ever loved him before and I will be such a better wife to him."

I was bargaining, not praying, but at the time it was all I knew. I had started to hear God knocking.

On day twenty, the doctor gave us the bad news. They had tried everything. There was nothing left. Nobody thought he could make it. They advised us to take him off life support.

This never sank in. My husband was *not* going to die. I didn't know at the time where my certainty came from, but God's knock was getting louder.

The doctors turned off my husband's life support system and pulled the tube from his throat. Then I saw it. I ran out to the waiting room, to my husband's brother and sisters: "He's breathing, he's breathing all on his own! God has answered everyone's prayers!" The doctors were never able to explain what happened. It became clear that this man had lived only by the grace of God.

Shortly after we were home and all the commotion had died down, I woke up one morning to hear God not only knocking but ringing my doorbell as well! He was saying, "You have your life back, now it is time to truly hand it over to me."

Suddenly, I saw His kindness. He had sent His only son to die for me; though my husband had never heard Him knocking, He had spared his life. Even though I did not know Him at all, He had blessed me with a wonderful life. He had then given me a second gift of not taking my husband away from me. I realized I had never been in control after all.

I began looking for a church that day and found one just like the little church my parents went to in West Virginia when I was a child. I am so comfortable there it is just like going home. I thank God every single day that He never stopped knocking on my door. I am not worried about how long it will take my husband to hear the knock. People are praying for it!

~ *Melissa Fields*

A Night up in Smoke

MY FRIEND DUSTY and I sat in my parents' basement, smoking marijuana and listening to the Rolling Stones album *Let It Bleed,* one of my favorites.

My parents gone for the weekend, I felt safe. The smell would be gone before they got home on Sunday. It was still Thursday. Lots of time to smoke dope, listen to music, and gab. Something was on my mind, though. I had just graduated from college a couple of months earlier. Dusty had turned twenty-four and still hadn't made it through any of the three schools he'd tried. He was drifting, and I felt concerned. I had to straighten him out.

Maybe I wanted to straighten Dusty out to keep my mind off myself. Deep down, a terror gripped me. Now that I'd finished college, I had to do something with my life. I had this general fear of the future. Who was I? Where was I going? What was I supposed to do with my life? I had this idea that someone—God, maybe—should come down and tell me: "Mark, you were meant to be a . . ." I could deal with whatever it was. *Just tell me,* my heart cried.

I asked Dusty what he planned to do in the days ahead.

"I don't know," he said. "Smoke pot and enjoy life."

"Do you believe in anything?" I asked casually. Not that I did. But over the last six months, I had been tinkering with thoughts about Christ. My friends, the Pezzis, had become Christians. I had come home the previous Christmas to find them fanatical about it. Over my last semester at Colgate University I'd prayed, read the Bible, and searched other books to learn more about religion. I hadn't come away with certain convictions about anything religious or Christian, just a vague idea that it could be important.

"What do you mean—believe?"

"You know, what are your beliefs?" I thought about it. "For instance, I know that I believe in music, and life, and having fun, and doing good things. I guess you could say I'm a lover of life. It's great to be alive. That's what I believe. Do you have anything like that?"

"Well, sure," he said, "I believe in that stuff. Maybe not as much, but I like living. Getting high is pretty good."

I felt frustrated. I knew he wasn't getting it. I finally blurted, "Do you believe in Jesus Christ or God?"

"I don't know. I never thought much about it, to tell you the truth." Then he turned the question around. "Do *you* believe in Christ?"

His question stunned me. Never had I ever been asked quite so baldly. I knew he would laugh at me if I said I did, too, and that struck me. Why didn't I just dodge the question like I usually did with such issues? What would it hurt? But somehow my answer mattered. I couldn't just laugh it off. I felt like I was in court, and my answer was the difference between life or death.

"Well?" Dusty asked.

"You know, I don't know why," I said, "but I believe that Jesus was the Son of God."

Dusty snickered. "To each his own," he said, and we turned to other subjects.

The next morning I woke up with a sense of pure excitement. I marveled at the sunlight, so pure and radiant. As I walked on the grass, laden with dew, my feet felt wonderful. *What is this?* I kept wondering, not sure of what was going on. Was I still high? Everything looked beautiful—the trees, the cars going by on the street, the people. People were astonishing. Each one unique. Each one a creation of God.

Suddenly I realized that all of this came to me from God. All of creation, everything I experienced, was from His hand. Instinctively, I began praying and talking to Jesus, telling Him how thrilled I was and what a wonder His world was, and how I knew I'd changed. I had no more craving for drugs, or alcohol, and I realized some of the things I'd done—stealing, lying, sexual dalliances—had to stop. But there seemed no condemnation, no guilt. Just a subtle recognition that I would no longer live like that.

As the weekend moved on, I picked up my Bible and began reading. There before me were words that once seemed foreign, vague, and meaningless. Now they unfolded, full of meaning and instruction. I marveled at how I knew it was true, the Word of God, and that I would make this book my lifetime study.

I couldn't wait to tell all my friends what had happened. Most of them thought it was nonsense. If they recognized something had happened to me, they still wouldn't budge in terms of expressing their own interest in this Lord I'd discovered. That was a hard blow. But I steadied myself and began the long journey toward learning, growth, and finding out who this God was that I'd fallen in love with.

Over the next few months, I felt a call to the ministry and my life's work was suddenly settled in a single swoop. The raw terror that had gripped me in those days after graduation had lifted. God was with me. He was in me. He would lead me every step of the way. No matter where I happened to go, He would be there. That was the grand thing about this Christ relationship, I realized. I no longer had to be afraid. I had been accepted by the only One who really mattered, and for the first time in my life I felt centered, alive and real.

I knew it would never go away. And it hasn't.

$\sim$ *Mark Littleton*

Forever Safe

IT WAS ALMOST midnight when my husband Rick and I got home from visiting relatives. Frank, the boyfriend of a young woman who had stayed with us until a few days before, sat in his parked truck on the street. "I wonder what Frank's doing here at this time of night."

"Take the kids to bed and I'll see what he wants," Rick replied. I put our daughters in bed and went back outside. Rick and Frank stood on the front lawn. What I saw gave me a sick feeling.

Frank was drunk and pointing a gun at Rick. "Where is she?" he demanded. "Where's my girlfriend?" I hoped he was just trying to scare us with an empty pistol. Then he fired into the air— *BLAM!* Again he fired into the air and then at the ground. Every muscle in my body quaked with fear—looking down the barrel of that revolver, hearing the thunderous crack of each bullet.

"Lord, please help us," I prayed silently, expecting someone to hear the commotion and call the police.

"Mommy!" It was our three-year-old, Kristi, at the front door.

"Put your kid to bed!" Frank demanded. From where he stood, Frank could see into our hallway and would know if I used the phone. I took Kristi to her room, dropped to my knees by her bed, and prayed for God's protection. At that same moment, Frank pointed the gun in Rick's face and pulled the trigger. It clicked on an empty cylinder.

Frank shouted at me from the yard. "Come back out here!" I didn't want him coming into the house, so I quickly returned, looking frantically up and down the street to see if help was on its way. I'd heard stories about people being so scared their knees were knocking. I learned knees really can knock when we're scared! I felt incredible fear, but I had an undeniable inner peace at the same time—a peace I had discovered as a teenager.

ONE OF MY earliest childhood memories was telling my mother, "I hate you!" Out of four children, I was the rebellious one. My mom and I just couldn't seem to get along. We went to church faithfully, but argued just as regularly. After one argument, I stood before the mirror and looked at my angry face. I saw the depth of my sin. I said aloud to the reflection, "You are so *ugly*!" Suddenly I wanted more than anything for the Lord Jesus Christ to take me as I was—ugly, angry, and all. I prayed earnestly in my heart, "Lord, I want to be able to do all things through You." It was as if a light came on inside of me too. I *knew* Jesus had accepted me—or I had accepted Him. Without really knowing what it meant, I wrote on that date on my calendar, "I was saved." Jesus Christ entered a fourteen-year-old's life that night, and I knew He was there.

Becoming an angel after fourteen years of devilry isn't the easiest process in the world. But God never left me. I learned that when I began a relationship with the Lord, it was like being reborn. Growth occurs much like that of a baby. I was fed by

God's Word—the Bible. I learned to communicate through prayer, and I got my socialization with other believers.

The Bible taught me that love and self-control are fruit of the Spirit of God living within me. Through God's Spirit, I developed love, respect, and appreciation for my mother. God also taught me my security through the knowledge that He will never leave or forsake me, and that I'll be with Him throughout all eternity. I need not fear death when it comes because I'll be safe forever.

That's why I felt peace that night on the front lawn, with Frank threatening our lives. One phrase kept going through my mind: "To be absent from the body and to be present with the Lord" (2 Corinthians 5:8). I knew that if Frank carried out his threats, I would immediately be in Jesus' presence.

Eventually Frank left. We never saw him again. But I felt afraid for days. I jumped when the doorbell rang and continually checked to make sure the truck didn't return. I was so exhausted with worry that I became physically sick.

My friends prayed for me and told me to read Psalm 91. God flooded me again with His overwhelming peace: My fear left and shut the door on its way out.

Jesus said, "I am the resurrection, and the life: he that believeth in me, though he were dead, yet shall he live" (John 11:25). I know that anything can happen to me at any time. I could walk out the door and never come home. But I know I'll be safe at "home" in heaven, with Jesus, forever.

~ *Jan Potter*

On the Trail to Truth

"ALLAH, ALMIGHTY! ALLAH, Almighty! Muhammad is a prophet of God. I am testifying that Muhammad is a prophet of God. Let's pray. Let's pray . . ." The voice cried on over the loud speaker, reminding me of my sorrow. I gazed out my bedroom window. The mosque, as always, obscured my view. With tears of fear trickling down my face, I felt in my heart that I could never earn my way into heaven.

I had studied the Koran for myself. I would never be able to follow all the rules or fulfill the requirements of a true Muslim. Of this, I was certain. But what were my options? My place of birth and my home was Baghdad, Iraq.

Saddam's regime had an influence not unlike the mentality of the Nazi doctrine. I was taught hate, anger, unforgiveness, intolerance, prejudice, arrogance, and ignorance. Even though my parents didn't agree with this kind of thinking, that is what I felt I learned from society.

Surviving in the Islamic culture was especially difficult for me. In my land, a physical handicap is considered a judgment from Allah. My slight limp brought on mistreatment—comments and scorn—from everyone from schoolteachers to passersby on the street. My world seemed very dark and hopeless. The more sadness and violence I saw, the more I questioned.

I wondered if this was the best and true way to live. Seeing the dead bodies of "traitors" hanging from lampposts in the city square made me sick, and eventually, I grew tired of trying to convince myself and others that Islam was a peaceful religion. Most Muslims do not allow themselves to think that leaving Islam is a possibility, but the Holy Spirit was planting that seed of thought in my mind.

Saddam had stripped my hard-working father of his position and possessions. However, my father persevered. He started a new business in Denmark and sent my family money. When I was old enough, he sent me to the United States for a college education. At the university, I became friends with other Muslims from the Middle East. I called myself a Muslim, but I wasn't practicing any of the religion's doctrine. I buried myself in my studies during the week and escaped troubling thoughts by partying on the weekends.

Looking back on those days, I know God was protecting me. He was saving me from myself. Matter of fact, I can see how the Spirit of God was with me and never left me throughout my earlier life. I don't know how He reached me, but I know He was drawing me to Himself. I was bound by fear and lost in darkness, but He was preparing a way for me to find the truth.

After graduation, I found a good job. There at work, I met a kind man named Kevin whom I eventually married. When I gave birth to our son, Joshua, my heart cried out for something more in life. Kevin had no religious background and I was a non-practicing Muslim, so we had decided early in our marriage to avoid spiritual discussions. Yet, I had a deep desire for Joshua to be safe and secure. I somehow believed that a spiritual connection was what he would need to give his life a real purpose.

I had my husband take Joshua to a mosque, but after a few visits I felt very uneasy about them going. I realized that if I wasn't convinced that the Islamic faith was good and true and meaningful to me, I shouldn't expose my young son to it.

This began our hunt for another faith and religious experience. For about three years, we tried church after church. Any denomination would do. We were hungry for the time and attention of someone who might give us spiritual attention and lead us to real answers to our growing questions.

I remember how desperately we wanted to belong. Every time we visited a new church, we wondered if this would be the place where someone would reach out to us and help us find our way. We were wandering in the wilderness, and we went down a lot of false trails.

By now, my son was a preschooler. The school my neighbors recommended was held at a Protestant church. Little Joshua soon came home from school full of new ideas. He talked about Jesus as if He was his new best friend. He wanted to pray at mealtimes and bedtime. With Joshua's encouragement, Kevin and I decided to visit the church, and after attending the church one Sunday, our family received a letter from the pastor, a phone call from a church member, and a visit from a couple of people.

As the people from this church told me about Jesus Christ and His sacrifice on the cross for our sins, something resonated in my heart, telling me this was the truth. I learned that God loved me enough to send His son to die for me. God knew I could never be perfect or live up to a set of rules as the Koran commanded.

I entered a personal relationship with Jesus Christ in January of 2001. That September, I was baptized to symbolize the change that had come into my heart. I had never felt such an awesome combination of peace and exhilaration. Everything was new and wonderful. I was thankful and humbled that God had led me to Himself and His church through my son.

I became involved in church activities, volunteer work in the church office, and most importantly Bible study. I studied Scripture as though my life depended on it. Every week I came to Bible study class with all my homework done, all the answers written out in my workbook, and more questions to ask. I loved hearing the stories of the Old Testament and eagerly told my new friends what God was teaching me through His Word.

This time of becoming familiar with my Bible would soon prove providential in my life. The American involvement in the Iraqi conflict was escalating. Since the terrorist attacks in New York and Washington, D.C., that had happened the month of my baptism, I had avidly watched the news with increasing concern.

This war touched me personally. My family, friends, and other Iraqis were being killed. I became so upset that I pushed my Bible away. For me, the ground battle also became a spiritual battle. Who or what could I trust?

This was my first test as a Christian. At first I felt unexplained fear, anger, hurt, and emptiness. Finally I realized that I was still reacting to events as I had before I had Christ in my life. The Lord soon guided me to open my Bible again. I read, "Ye shall know the truth, and the truth shall make you free" (John 8:32). I was touched by the Holy Spirit's presence and I again felt peace. The Bible is still my constant companion, and it is the first place I go when troubles and trials come my way.

I am now seeking to live ever in closer relationship with Jesus. I found the strength and courage to witness to my mother and one of my brothers, both Muslims. Amazingly, they have not disowned me for becoming a Christian, as is common in the Muslim faith and culture. I have tried to be an example of Christian love to my friends and neighbors. My friends and family tell me that I am different—a better person. I smile because I know the truth—it is this relationship with Jesus that has made me better.

At first I felt alone on the trail of Truth, but as my husband and son and I have gotten involved in our church, God has graciously provided brothers and sisters in Christ for me to travel with. Through other Christians and God's Word, Jesus has taught me tolerance, empathy, compassion, humbleness, thankfulness, and forgiveness. I will be forever grateful that the Lord never forgot me, but led me from the darkness into the light of the Gospel. As He promised in Matthew 7:7, "Ask and it will be given to you; seek, and ye shall find; knock and the door will be opened unto you." Jesus set me free. In Matthew 19:26 I read that with man this isn't possible, but with God all things are possible. God's Word is truth on my journey of life.

～ Suha Gibson, as told to Evangeline Beals Gardner

No Longer Adrift

THE HEAVY AROMA of sandalwood incense set the scene for an evening of self-analysis and self-discovery. With candles as our only light, we three college couples sat in a cross-legged circle. We looked forward to the hard work of self-actualization and committed to do it for as long as it took to become new and improved happy people. In the weeks and months ahead our problems, conflicts, and painful pasts would all be resolved, and all of us in our small circle of friends would forge ahead in our married lives.

"Just spill your guts," urged our session leader. A bottle of homemade wine helped loosen our minds and lubricate our tongues so we could vocalize our innermost turmoil and deepest yearnings. As it turned out, however, self-actualization did nothing to change our conflicts, problems, or our painful pasts. Within a decade, we had racked up three divorces and great sadness. Six lives sailed adrift.

I had been anchored once. I'd grown up attending Sunday school and church, and my social life centered there. In my early dating days, my parents only allowed church-related activities. I believed in God, but the belief ran shallow. My life leaned more to fun than anything else.

My family moved when I turned fifteen. I tested the local church but didn't like the youth group, so I quit going. Since I'd never dug deep to see what God was all about, and since church was only a Sunday thing, I thought I could walk away and still be okay. I hadn't murdered anyone and I was a good person, so I figured Heaven would welcome me when my time came.

Right after high school graduation, a friend asked, "Want to go to church with me?"

"Sure, why not," I agreed. It sounded interesting, something different, and it was an easy half-mile walk from my house. At this church, the minister wore no robes. The congregation stood and belted out songs I'd never heard. They talked a lot about Jesus, too. They said they knew Him and had a relationship with Him. I felt uncomfortable. Thankfully, I liked the youth group and stayed on. One Sunday morning I responded to the weekly altar call and walked to the front of the church. I acknowledged I needed forgiveness and only God could save me. I came away believing I was now His child. I had entered that personal relationship with Jesus that they all spoke of.

Along with several young people from the congregation, I attended a Midwestern Bible college. I met a man who didn't honor God, but romantic love overshadowed my love for God, and I left school during my second year to become his wife. Perhaps that's when I began to go adrift.

Just four years after becoming a believer in Jesus Christ, I found myself in that candlelit living room, trying to solve my problems with self-actualization and human wisdom. Lack of spiritual commitment and buying into the counterculture's message pulled me perilously off course. While on that detour, I created my own "Ology Theory"—theology, psychology, astrology all worked together, interwoven parts of the same message.

A few years later I had a family of five and a different life-style. We owned a large home in a suburban neighborhood where the men toted attaché cases and drove off daily to their places of business, while the women toted diaper bags and sippy cups and drove their younger children to preschool, then served as room mothers for the older ones.

From the outside it appeared a recipe for happiness, an anchor of security, but inside our wedded walls were crumbling.

"I want to be happy—elsewhere," my husband announced one day. Our marriage disintegrated.

Alone with three children under age six, I found that life made no sense and held little purpose. My kids kept me going, but a mighty slim thread tethered me to sanity. I smiled by day and cried by night.

"Mind if I come over for a while?" I frequently asked friends on the other end of the telephone. Girlfriends listened to my agony and plied me with coffee and Kleenex. One of those girl-friends invited me to her church. Desperate for help, I loaded the kids in the station wagon and followed her to a round building where more than a thousand folks congregated, some in jeans and sandals. They sang choruses instead of hymns and talked even more about an intimate relationship with God and Jesus. In spite of its size, a sense of warmth pervaded the gathering and I felt safe. When the tears flowed, people didn't ignore me or step away as if I were diseased. Compassionate strangers put an arm around my shoulders, prayed with me, and suggested I call the church office to seek free counseling help.

I found a new path. Before my marriage ended, I had started a vague walk back to God, but with the shattering of my life, my slow walk became a mad dash and a do-or-die plunge into the safe waters of this church. The children plugged into two weekly Bible clubs, one after school and one at church, and I sought solace in a women's Bible study.

These women were an eclectic group who sported designer labels or Goodwill finds, held hard-earned college degrees or quickly achieved GEDs, and bore hearts and souls wrapped in pale pinkish or deep ebony skin. Yet they united in their love for God and the Bible, which they called the Word of God.

I discovered prayer wasn't just a listing in the church bulletin or a bedtime exercise, but an ongoing conversation with God, my Lord and my Father. God tested my new concept of prayer one evening.

I had tucked my children into their beds and retreated to my room. The ever-present tears flowed, and I knew the anguish building up over the past several months would destroy me if I didn't act. My emotions escalated, and I soon raged with hurt and fury. I curled on my bed and railed at God, screaming my despair about my pointless, drifting, lonely life. Frightened and half expecting instant divine retribution, I drew my knees tighter to my chest. I whispered, "God, I don't want to stay this way."

In that moment the anger and tension abated, and a sense of deep-rooted peace took hold. My heart unknotted. I knew my children and I would be all right.

I hurried to Bible study the next day, eager to tell the women that I could talk to God anytime, about everything. They smiled.

"He's God the Creator," I said, "but he's also like a daddy who invites me to crawl into His lap. It's really cool!" I laughed. "He's majestic, like thunder and power and so awesome. But other times it's as if I can take His hand, and we can go for a walk and just talk."

The study leader chuckled. "You're catching on, Lynn."

And I kept catching on.

My life came back on course, though I realized it wouldn't be an easy road. The rigorous life of single motherhood lay ahead, and I knew that even if I remarried, that would bring its own set of challenges. But even though the storms do come, I don't feel like I'm adrift anymore. Christ has not just become my personal savior, He's become my anchor, to keep me stable and on the right course in the channel of life.

∼ Lynn Ludwick

Change of Heart

"DAD, WHO MADE God? Where did He come from?" I remember asking these questions at the ripe old age of five.

As my father looked down at me, I saw a glint of either pride or amazement that such a small kid could ask such a question. Believe me, it wasn't because I was a genius. Something more motivated my question. For some reason, I couldn't stand who I was or how I felt.

Going to church in the rural Texas town where we lived was a habit, if not a concrete expectation—twice on Sunday and once on Wednesday evening. I couldn't stand it. In fact, I couldn't stand any of the other kids or my Sunday school teacher. I thought they were stupid and couldn't get the stories right. One Sunday, before I realized the words were actually escaping my mouth, I blurted out to a girl in my class, "You're stupid!"

I couldn't let it rest there and proceeded to let my Sunday school teacher know that she didn't know what she was talking about. I mean, everybody in their right minds knew that Jonah was swallowed by a big fish—not a whale! That just went too far, especially after last Sunday's messed-up story about Moses.

"And besides that, what's with all this stupid cutting and pasting of Bible people pictures? That isn't fun. You're wasting my time." This behavior was relayed to my parents, changing the glint in my father's eye. He tried to suppress disappointment, embarrassment, and anger—a look I will never forget and have tried to avoid causing since.

After enduring what seemed like an eternal scolding and subsequent whooping, I thought church people were still some pretty stupid folks. This attitude bled over to how I acted with my cousins, schoolmates, friends, everyone. I felt a consistent nagging that wouldn't go away. It was small at first, but it gradually increased to the point where I just wanted to rip it out of my mind and heart. I didn't know how or what to do—that is, until I told Mom and Dad. "I don't like myself. I don't like being mad all the time. I hate feeling guilty."

I knew the story about Jesus being crucified on the cross, but my heart didn't change until one night when Mom read a routine bedtime story. The words "Believe in your heart" popped in my head and I said them out loud.

"What did you say?" Mother asked.

"Believe in your heart."

"Those words are in the Bible, Kurt. Did you know that?"

"No."

"Here, let's look them up. They're found in Romans, Chapter 10, verses 9 and 10. These scriptures tell us that if we confess with our mouths that Jesus is Lord, and you believe in your heart that God's raised him from the dead, you'll be saved."

Mother explained why Jesus died for me—because He loved me, taking all the bad things I'd done in His own body, causing Him to die. But He came back to life, so He could forgive me and take me to heaven when I die. I began to understand that He was my answer.

Dad came in, and he and Mom sat on my little bed as they led me through a prayer to God. "I know I have been bad and I'm sorry for being mean, but please forgive me and let Jesus, Your Son, come and live in my heart. I don't want to be like I am now. I want to change. I want a different heart. I want to love. I want You."

Immediately I started bawling. Something was different inside me. I felt so happy and confused and couldn't understand it, but I didn't care. I felt joy and wanted everyone to know it. I'd never used the telephone before, but for the next half hour, I told both sets of grandparents, "Jesus is in my heart!"

Little did I know this was only the beginning of my crying out for God to change my heart.

When I was sixteen, I applied to attend the United States Military Academy at West Point. During the physical screening process, the doctors discovered I had a heart murmur and enlarged left ventricle. We got this condition cleared after paying for a few more tests to confirm I was fit to be a part of the military. In February of 1990, I signed the green postcard letting the academy know I would begin attending that July. I was now in control of my own destiny, I figured. God laughed.

West Point and the Hudson River are beautiful. But I didn't experience that beauty until my last week there. The rest of the time, I was stressed past what I thought was my breaking point, constantly afraid of not measuring up. However, after multiple daily prayers, losing part of my nose in boxing class, and nearly losing an eye, I graduated as a second lieutenant, commissioned in the field artillery in May 1994. This experience taught me a ton about myself, but I missed part of the lesson God was trying to get through my thick skull.

As a first lieutenant in the First Cavalry Division at Fort Hood, Texas, I began to find it harder and harder to recover after physical training. I chalked this up to getting "older" at the age of twenty-five. It wasn't until I wrecked my fiancée's pickup truck, flipping it a few times, that doctors discovered something wrong with my heart. I had been born with two, instead of three, leaflets in my aortic valve, and the root of the aorta was expanding. This allowed blood to flow both ways through the valve, causing my heart to work much harder.

Six months after getting married in 1997, I was given the option to have surgery to repair this valve immediately, or to wait a year or so, when I would have no choice but to have the surgery. *What a way to start a marriage. Let's scare her and possibly die.* I hated the thought of putting my wife through that.

"I won't let circumstances control my life. I'll beat it to the punch, have the surgery, fight back into shape, and show everyone how I'm still in control," I announced. Of course I consulted God about what to do and tried to rely on Him. But again, I missed part of His lesson. And again, He laughed.

I am now thirty-four years old and asking, "How many times does God need to whack me in the head with a two-by-four for me to realize I am not in control?" I am now scheduled for surgery again—for the same procedure. The homograft, or human tissue valve, that God allowed me to use these past nine years has worn out. I will get a mechanical valve this time, hopefully extending the life of my heart for another twenty to thirty years. Even though I've made a series of choices leading to an awesome marriage, a successful management career, and a master's degree, it's taken me this long to understand I don't even want to be in control of my life—and actually, I never have been in control.

Surgery like this has caused me to pause and reflect on what I've done and haven't yet done. God started to draw me closer to Him even before I realized what was happening to me physically. Along with a physical heart, I truly believe the Great Physician is still working on replacing my spiritual heart. I've been a born-again Christian since I was five, but I'm just now learning how to love others the way I should. Kind of sad that God has to repeatedly whoop my rear end before I actually catch on. But then I've never been accused of being bright—just ornery.

Instead of turning to God only when the going gets a bit bumpy or even rough, I'm learning to work with Him along the entire way by trusting and having faith in His control—not mine.

The question of who made God is still a good one, but one I now know cannot be answered or understood fully by us humans. It is a question I don't need an answer to because I know He exists and have seen His grace—in sunrises and sunsets, in the smell of rain, in an eagle's wings, in old married couples holding hands . . . and in my heart.

~ Kurt A. Miesner

Editors' note: As this book is going to press, Kurt has gone through surgery in which some calcified arteries were removed and he was given a mechanical valve. He has just been transferred out of ICU, and his prognosis looks great.

Drawn by Love

THE THIRD ONE'S a charm, they say, and Kevin was proving them to be right.

Kevin Pratt was the third Kevin I had dated, but he was different from my former boyfriends, and from anyone else I had ever met. While other people I met at college seemed driven by parties and promiscuity, Kevin wasn't. Instead, he had a kindness and gentleness about him that drew me to him. I wanted to see what made him the man he was.

As we got to know each other better, Kevin told me he was a Christian. I was raised Catholic and was glad to know that we shared a belief in the same God — Father, Son, and Holy Spirit in one. I was secretly troubled, though, by Kevin's strong faith and the peace he drew from it.

I had struggled with my own faith for years. In my mind, God was a big eye in the sky watching for any misstep on my part. If I did something wrong, He would surely punish me. I believed I needed to work for His love and the chance to spend eternity with Him in heaven. I needed to be good.

But no matter what I did, I never felt good enough. In high school, I had confessed these feelings of spiritual inadequacy to my priest, and he had replied, "You're trying too hard to be perfect."

I had left the confession booth feeling more confused: Did I stand a better chance of going to heaven by being less perfect?

Now, as Kevin and I drew closer, I wondered if I was treading into even deeper spiritual quicksand. I kept thinking, *Marrying a man outside my church may lessen my chances of making it into heaven.*

But I loved Kevin and he loved me. The only solution I saw was that one of us had to give—and it wasn't going to be me! I figured I needed to hurry up and make him believe as I did. When he asked me to marry him, I laid my spiritual focus on the line and cut to the chase.

"I'm Catholic," I told him, "and I'm never going to change, so we're going to have to marry in the Catholic Church."

Knowing that he considered himself a Protestant Christian and cherished his beliefs, I expected a standoff. But Kevin surprised me once again with his gentleness. He agreed to marry in my church and even agreed to attend it with me to get to know it better and keep us together Sunday mornings.

Kevin began visiting with a priest from a parish close to his home to learn more, and he soon invited me along. During the visit, I became agitated when I realized this priest viewed the Catholic Church and its teachings differently than I did. He kept telling me, "You need to put all of your trust in Jesus." His words made no sense! I refused to go back to that priest.

After we married, Kevin continued to be a kind, sweet husband. A few times when the subject arose, he'd honestly tell me that I couldn't improve my chances of getting into heaven by clinging to cloths that had been blessed or by other symbols of my religion. As I lived with this man, I knew he had something I didn't. Perhaps as part of the love and peace I sensed in his life,

I was soon desperate to find the answers to the spiritual yearnings inside of my own life. Every night I prayed for a miracle to show me the way to find peace with God.

Unknown to me, at that time and just on the other side of the bed, Kevin was also praying for a miracle for me—only he was praying that I would experience a relationship with God by coming to know Jesus Christ rather than just experiencing a religion.

One night I had a dream in which I was told, "Love Jesus with all of your heart." In my dream, I had no response, and the voice repeated, "Love Jesus with all of your heart." The troubling dream kept replaying, gaining intensity. Finally I blurted out, "I can't. I don't know Jesus."

I woke up, cold, on the verge of tears, my heart pounding. The only person I thought might understand what I had just experienced was Kevin, but I didn't dare tell him—I wasn't ready to admit that my religion lacked the main ingredient: Jesus.

Only a few days later, Kevin asked me if I would read the Bible with him every night before going to bed. The times I had tried to read the Bible, it had appeared to be a bunch of boring mumbo-jumbo, but I said yes to make him happy.

I remember reading that God's Word goes out and always accomplishes God's purposes. Still, most of what Kevin and I read didn't make sense to me, and I didn't feel as if I was getting anything out of reading the Bible.

Then one morning I woke up with the feeling of a hand resting on my shoulder. I looked around, but no one was in the room. Kevin was shuffling around in the bathroom, getting ready for work. The warmth of the hand flowed through my body and a soft voice said, "I'm a loving God. I'm a kind God. I'm a gentle God."

I felt an enormous peace I had never felt before. I knew I was in the presence of God, and I didn't want him to leave me. His words had wiped out every preconceived idea I had of who God was.

Still, I couldn't tell Kevin. *I'm not charismatic. Why are all of these strange things happening to me?* I wondered. Kevin was Lutheran, another old mainline church tradition that didn't normally hear voices in dreams or feel non-existent hands on shoulders. I was afraid if I told my new husband about these experiences he'd think I was going crazy.

After this last incident, I became so consumed with all of the strange things happening to me that I had difficulty sleeping. One night, when I couldn't fall asleep, I started praying. I was suddenly hit by all the wrong I had done in life, and I began to sob. I spent more than an hour laying out all of my wrongs to God, talking to Him through prayer and crying.

Basically, I was repenting of my sins without knowing I was repenting. I had never truly understood what *repentance* meant. Feeling broken, I lifted one of my hands toward heaven and told God, "Take my hand and lead me. Take my life. I'm yours. I can't do it anymore."

This time, I couldn't *not* tell Kevin. I woke him and relayed what had just happened.

He leaped out of bed with a shout of "Hallelujah!" and told me he had been praying for me, and this moment, since the days we had dated. He suggested we read the Bible together. As we read words from the Bible, I understood them for the first time. It was as if I had been wearing a veil that now was lifted.

I was amazed at how the Holy Spirit had led me through the steps of becoming a believer—acknowledging my sins and

God as the only one who could save me from the consequences for them, asking for forgiveness, and inviting Jesus into my life—without my even knowing what those steps were. No one else had told me those steps, although my husband had prayed faithfully that I would take them. God had used a gentle, praying husband and my voracious desire for spiritual truth to reach me with his love.

~ Kelli Pratt, as told to Ronica Stromberg

The Voice of the Future

"OKAY, THAT'S ALL now. You can pay me and go," the fortune-teller said, abruptly dropping my hand. But fear filled my heart. I could tell by her guarded expression that this wasn't all.

When I'd apprehensively arrived at Ms. Gasket's Gothic-style house in the old part of the city, she hadn't looked as I'd expected. She was a tiny Caucasian woman in her late sixties or early seventies. She looked totally drained, with light blue eyes that seemed to see through to my soul.

Ms. Gasket went about her craft, looking into my palms; she turned both hands over and scrutinized them. Grimacing, she said, "Your life has been interrupted twice. You should have been dead a long time ago."

"Yes, you're right," I'd said. I told her how I was raped at knifepoint and probably would have been killed, but I had heard a voice tell me to get up and run. That same year I had interrupted a burglary and barely escaped with my life.

Ms. Gasket then predicted several things about my future — she said I'd move to another state, get divorced, get remarried, and change careers.

"That's all," she now repeated.

"What did you see? You saw something else, didn't you?" I demanded nervously.

"People want to hear the good things," she said with a frown, "but they don't want to hear about the bad things."

"Ms. Gasket, I've come this far. Tell me what you saw," I insisted.

She looked at me sternly. "Are you sure?" she asked.

I swallowed the lump in my throat and said, "Sure."

"You will not live to see your thirty-eighth birthday," Ms. Gasket intoned. "You should not be living now. I don't know what's going on, but a black cloud is over your life. I'm sorry," she finished.

I had always been curious about my future. When I was in college, I became interested in horoscopes and even paid to have my astrological chart compiled. A few years later, my friend Cecilia had told me about a psychic whose predictions always seemed to come true. I was all ears! We talked with others who had actually visited this lady. One coworker told us, "She is a real prophet. She told me I would marry a wealthy man, and it happened like she said."

After months of careful consideration, Cecilia and I had gone to see her. I had waited anxiously in the sitting room while Cecilia met with Ms. Gasket. I wondered what they were doing in there. I'd always equated fortunetellers with witches and warlocks, but surely she wouldn't put a spell on me or anything. *No, that's a silly thought,* I decided. But I still wondered if I was consorting with the devil.

I'd given my life to God as an eleven-year-old at the little church on the corner near our home. My father had grown up as the son of a fire-and-brimstone Baptist preacher, but he left home at an early age to escape from all the preaching. Neither of my parents cared much about God when I was a girl, and church attendance wasn't pressed. Since I rarely attended church, my early seed of faith just withered. Thinking back, I remembered wanting to know about my life and future even then.

Now, returning to that sitting room, I was dazed, absorbing what she'd said. *I'm going to die young?* Is this what my quest for knowledge had led me to? Maybe I was not supposed to know the future. Cecilia and I left, vowing never to tell anyone of our experience.

I was twenty-five years old when I received that reading. I never went back to another palm reader, fortuneteller, or "prophet." The years passed. I got divorced, moved out of state, and remarried—all Ms. Gasket's predictions were coming true. The words "You will not live to see your thirty-eighth birthday" haunted my mind for the next thirteen years. But I continued to live. I would not let some prediction rule my life.

Finally, my thirty-eighth birthday came—and went. When the day was over, I sighed with relief and said, "Well, Ms. Gasket, you missed this one."

A week later, I was leaving work to get some lunch. I got into my little green Chevy and stopped at a red light outside my office building. When the light turned green, I proceeded through the intersection. *Pow!* A speeding construction truck ran the red light and broadsided my car on the driver's side.

As the car spun out of control, I screamed, "Help!" Then I realized that this was it—the final prediction was coming true. *I'm going to die,* I thought.

I couldn't get control of my car as it headed toward a light pole. Then I heard a voice say, *"I have dominion over life and death."* The moment I heard those words my car stopped abruptly, almost as if on command, just inches from the light pole. I heard people out on the sidewalk calling for help and running to my car. They tried to pull me out on the driver's side, but it was smashed like a soda can.

An ambulance arrived, and the paramedics pulled me from the passenger's side. Half conscious, I heard one of my coworkers ask, "Is she going to live?"

The next thing I remember was being in the hospital, lying on a cold steel gurney, in excruciating pain. I heard doctors talking about me.

"Apparently her car was totally smashed. It's a wonder she's alive."

"Ma'am, are you all right?"

"We can't give you any medication right now. We have to take the glass out of your arm—do you understand?"

"Yes," I mumbled.

The doctors seemed oblivious to my moans as they chatted about work and other personal matters while pulling glass shards from my arm. Hot tears trickled down my cheeks and warm blood rolled down my back. The pain was unbearable. Then I heard, *"This is how my blood rolled down my back for you."* I was in distress, but I distinctly heard a voice speaking in my spirit. I stopped moaning long enough to focus on that voice. It was the same voice I'd heard at other crucial times in my life. I wanted to find out more about that voice. *Someone is watching over me,* I thought.

When I was released from the hospital, I had one goal: to find that Voice, and the One who seemed to be watching over me. Before the accident, I didn't think seriously about eternal life. I was skeptical and confused. My experience with some so-called Christians didn't show me a difference between saved and unsaved, holy and unholy. They partied alongside me, a rank sinner. I remember saying to a friend, "I won't 'play church.' Either I will be a true Christian or I won't, but I won't play with God." I didn't know exactly how to go about finding the Voice, but I knew how to pray.

I began repenting of my sins in the privacy of my walk-in closet at home. Every morning I would get up very early, go to my closet, and seek God. I do not know how many days I performed this ritual. But I wanted to be sure that *He* knew I was repentant, and that I wanted to be saved. One morning during my prayers, I invited Jesus into my life. When I walked out of the closet that morning, I knew I would never be the same. I can't describe it, but I felt different. It was as if a weight had been lifted. I felt cleansed, refreshed, and renewed. I had been born again!

I seemed to be bursting at the seams. I was so happy, I couldn't keep this to myself—I had to tell somebody. I returned to the church I'd attended occasionally before my accident to share my good news. I was saved! I was forgiven of my sins—past, present, and future!

Knowing about my future had been my life's pursuit. Now I no longer desire to know my future because I know it is secure with the one who knows me—the one who used to be a Voice, but is now my personal Lord.

～ *B. J. Leffall-McGibboney*

Clean at Last: Inside and Out

"HEY ED,* YOU'D better clean house. The word on the street is that the cops have their sights on you."

I'd been getting these kinds of warnings here and there that my nice little drug business was about to go south. Out in the drug world, I was a big shot. Yet when I lay in my bed at night, alone in the darkness, I knew what I was doing was wrong. My $600-a-day cocaine habit was catapulting me down the road to disaster. I'd gotten to the point where I did cocaine from the time I got up in the morning until I passed out at night. The pressure of working seventy hours a week, doing drugs, and dealing was becoming more than I could handle. Now, the cops were after me. How did I ever get into such a mess?

People say when you're about to die, your life flashes before you. Maybe I wasn't dying, but that night I saw the scenes of my life, and it was like a horror movie in living color . . .

"Ed, I'm sorry, but your Dad died today." My mother did her best to comfort my older sister, Lil, my younger brother, Jake,

*All names have been changed.

and me over the news. Dad had been sick with a rare nerve disease for several years. After his death, when I was seventeen, I started experimenting with marijuana to try to deaden the pain and fill the gnawing emptiness inside of me.

Mom found a boyfriend and got wrapped up in her own life. One day Mom and Jack went through a messy break-up in our living room. A gunshot rang out.

"Oh, no! He's shot Mom!" my sister screamed. "Quick, call for help!" I picked up the phone, but it was too late. Now both of our parents were gone.

After Mom's death, my dabbling in drugs took a quantum leap into cocaine use. I began dealing and worked my way up in the organization. Street dealing was not my thing—I sold to the guys who broke the cocaine into smaller quantities and then distributed it to the street dealers. Every weekend, the kids on the block gathered at our house, and we did some serious partying.

Later a church purchased an old mansion behind our house. The building not only provided space for the church but also housed several families from the congregation. Before long they discovered "the house on the hill" was the scene of some very loud, wild parties. Some of our partiers had a confrontation with a couple of guys from the mansion, Steve and Mike. We didn't know it, but Steve and Mike began praying for the kids at the house on the hill. They felt badly about the argument and asked God to give them an opportunity to share Jesus with us.

Then my sister came home one day with interesting news. "Hey, Ed, one of the guys from that crazy church next door is painting my car. The insurance company sent me over to his shop. I have to pick up the car next Saturday." Lil got more than she bargained for when she picked up her car. Steve shared how much Jesus loved her and wanted to give her a new life. She broke down in tears, realizing this was the answer to the void in her heart. Lil was a different person after that day. She began going to the church, getting involved in activities, and telling her brothers about Jesus.

"Now, Lil, just leave me alone," I told her. "I'm not interested in that religious stuff." But my big sister kept praying for me while I kept brushing her off. For five years, the nightmare of my life continued. One morning I got up and began pacing the floor, memories tormenting me. I'd had so many close calls with drug deals going bad. Even my boys could not have protected me. I knew my sister's prayers had something to do with my survival.

As I thought of Lil and her newfound joy, I began to want what she had. Everything was crumbling around me. My life was lonely, even though my house was usually filled with people. I began to cry out to God. Since my sister wasn't home, I thought maybe if I went to her room I could find what she had. In utter defeat and hopelessness, I sat on her bed and sobbed.

That evening, Steve drove Lil home from a church meeting. "I hear someone crying," Lil said. Recalling the way Mom was killed, Lil was afraid to venture to her room alone. She and Steve found me lying on her bed.

"Hey, brother, what's wrong?" Lil asked in alarm.

"Lil, I need whatever it is you have. I can't go on like this." I choked as I tried to explain.

"Ed, you can have a brand-new life in Jesus Christ," said Lil.

"I'm a junkie and a dealer. Why would He want me?" I just couldn't imagine anyone, much less God, caring about me in my present condition.

"None of us deserves God's love," Steve said. "But Jesus died for everyone. Do you want to ask His forgiveness and turn your life over to Him?"

I nodded my agreement.

"Just repeat this prayer after me: Jesus, I know I'm a sinner. I ask that you would forgive me. I give you my life this day. Help me turn away from drugs and drug dealing. Amen."

I prayed the prayer with Steve, and that night I went to bed and slept peacefully. And something happened that I can't explain. I woke up with no desire for cocaine, no need for it, and no withdrawal. It was like my life up to that point had been one giant nightmare, and now the nightmare was over. I cleaned house—no more drugs or dealing. The dark characters who had supplied me with drugs never bothered me again. The cops didn't beat down my door. It was just over. I've met many people since then who say that's a miracle. For most people, it takes some time to get out of the web of addiction and all its problems.

I went to church with Lil the next Sunday. The people there stepped into the gap left by the death of our folks and became like moms and dads to us. With all I had been through, I now wanted to help other young people avoid the traps I had fallen into. After taking a course, I became a Scoutmaster. I also met my wife in church, and God blessed us with two beautiful children.

My parents died, leaving me an orphan. Yet by God's grace, I've been adopted into His family and set free from drugs and a hopeless life.

~ *Ed Stevenson, as told to Susan J. Reinhardt*

God and the Marriage Mess

HOW DID I get into this mess? Why did I marry this man? I wondered. We'd just had our worst fight yet. I peered out my bedroom window to make sure our four-year-old daughter, Jenn, was okay as she skated on the sidewalk outside of our apartment.

Marlo didn't seem to understand how lonely I was. He was stationed with the army at Schofield Barracks in Hawaii. I'd never lived an ocean away from family and friends. I felt like I was on a deserted island. My husband had his work and buddies to occupy his time, but I had two small children and no one to talk to.

I'd tried to make him understand. "Marlo, you leave for work before sunup, then come home at five and have the audacity to say you're going for a bike ride? What about family time?"

"What about it?" he said. "I'll be back. Besides, I need time for myself."

"What about me? When do I get time for myself?"

"Are you saying that I can't have free time? Boy, if I knew it was going to be like this, I wouldn't have gotten married."

"Things change when you have a family, Marlo!"

"Who says they have to change? I don't like you telling me what I can and can't do!"

Before we had gotten married, Marlo always kept busy. Besides his daytime duties at work, he regularly took "charge of quarters" duty, which is overnight, as well as attending various parties given by other soldiers. He played on his unit's baseball team, which required daily practices and games once or twice a week. And he trained daily for triathlons around nearby cities. All of this was on top of his frequent field training.

But now that he had a wife and children, I expected Marlo to be there for us, especially since we were adjusting to our new home.

Marlo knocked on the door. "Liza, can we talk?"

"No! I'm finished talking. I have nothing more to say," I announced.

Christy, our eight-month-old daughter, squealed in the next room, and Marlo went to get her. I looked out the window again and noticed a couple talking to Jenn. The woman had a baby about Christy's age in a stroller. The man picked up the baby and held her close while he kissed her gently on the forehead. After talking with Jenn, they walked into an apartment.

Later that evening I headed outdoors for a stroll with Jenn and Christy. We ran into the woman who had talked to Jenn earlier. "It's Miss Belinda, Mommy! Hi, Miss Belinda!" Jenn cried.

Belinda and I exchanged introductions. This simple meeting eventually led to many visits, as Belinda took me under her wing. Her husband was a naval officer stationed at Pearl Harbor. She didn't seem to care that my husband was only an enlisted soldier in the army. Belinda was different than anyone I was used to. She was confident, yet gentle. She spoke kind words and behaved very much like a lady. Although our apartments were identical in structure, hers felt peaceful, serene, and safe. Over the next month, we became fast friends. We visited frequently, talking about our hobbies, jobs we held, and baby stuff. She invited me over for lunch two to three times a week. I occasionally baby-sat her daughter, and she sometimes watched my girls.

Then Belinda and her family moved to Pearl City, about eight miles from our apartment. Although she promised to keep in touch, I never expected to hear from her again. Two weeks passed without a word. Finally, to my surprise, Belinda called and invited me to lunch.

At that point I had no idea that Belinda had prayed for me long before we met. She had asked God to send her someone who needed Him. And that person had turned out to be me.

Belinda always seemed to know exactly what I needed. Whether it was food, encouraging words, or information on treating a certain illness, she had a way of fulfilling that need before I could even say anything. She talked to me about marriage and her role as wife in their home. As our relationship grew, I opened my heart to her. I described the struggles in my marriage, the problems I'd had while growing up, and my challenges with Marlo's overbearing family. I told her how scared and lonely I felt.

"I stay awake half the night when Marlo's in the field because I hate being alone at night. When he's home, I rarely get help from him. I'm exhausted. I don't know whether I'm better off with him gone or with him home. All we do is fight." Gradually I even told her the deepest secret in my heart . . . that my greatest fear was of dying.

Belinda listened attentively, not saying a word. When I finished, she rose and went into her dining room. She came back with a Bible.

Great, I thought. What's she going to do with that? Preach a sermon?

"Liza, would you say that you know God?"

"I don't know what you mean," I said. "Is it really possible to really know God?"

"Absolutely. Let's start with your fear of dying. Why do you suppose you're afraid?"

"Because I've done some shameful things in my life, and maybe because I don't know what happens after death."

"Anyone who believes that Jesus is the Son of God, who died and rose again so we may have eternal life with the Father, will spend eternity in heaven." Then she quoted John 3:16: "For God so loved the world that he gave his only begotten son, that whosoever believeth in him should not perish but have everlasting life."

"Okay, Belinda, but I've done some things that not even God can forgive."

But she persisted. "God will not only forgive your unmentionable sins, but He will erase them like they never happened at all. In Psalm 103:11–12 he says he loves us so much that He takes our sins from us as far as the east is from the west. That means *all* your sins—not just the simple white lies, but *all* of them. You see, Paul in the Bible even murdered Christians, and yet he later gave his life to Christ and became a leader in telling others about Jesus."

I found it hard to believe that God could forgive all of my "little" wrongdoings, let alone the bigger sins. I'd always felt I was doomed. I wondered if I would ever have the peace Belinda exuded.

Over the following months I enjoyed learning about God and watching Belinda's every move as a mother and wife. After we had dinner together one evening, Belinda sat next to me on the sofa. I could hear our girls playing in the next room.

"Liza, we've learned quite a bit about God," she began. "Are you ready to put your trust in Him?"

I thought for a moment. What could I possibly lose from giving my life to Christ? I know Jesus was God's Son, and He died on the cross and rose again three days later. Out loud I said, "I believe I am."

So as the scent of plumeria trees wafted in through the open windows, in Belinda's living room, I recited the prayer of salvation. Immediately I knew something was different. Although Marlo was in the field at the time, I was not afraid of being alone at home. I had the assurance of knowing where I was going if I was to die. I couldn't remember ever feeling so calm and peaceful before.

Throughout the rest of our time together in Hawaii, Belinda taught me about being a godly wife and mother. She encouraged me to study the Bible and have quiet times with God.

I would like to say that God healed our marriage right away, but that wasn't the case. I thought our relationship was getting better, but on Christmas Eve Marlo asked for a divorce. He acknowledged that he had seen some good changes in my life, but as he sat in the overstuffed chair across from me, he announced that he was still unhappy and wanted out of the marriage. He gave me an ultimatum: "Either I get to do what I want to do, or I'm out the door. I'm not trying to change you, and you shouldn't try to change me."

He was partly right. I knew well enough that God was the only one who could change Marlo in the same way He was slowly changing me. On the other hand, I didn't want to have a husband who wanted to live like a single man, coming home whenever he pleased or letting his parents run us. So I held my ground and disagreed.

"Well, Liza," he said, "I have no choice but to ask for a divorce."

"Okay, Marlo, if that's what you want. But can I share one more thing with you that I learned from the Bible?"

"Go ahead. I'm listening."

"Genesis 2:24 says a man should leave his father and mother and become as one flesh with his wife."

Marlo didn't say anything. I could almost see the wheels turning in his head. As the truth sank in, he looked as if the wind had been knocked out of him, and soon after, a light came on. "What else does it say?"

So I read more passages to him about how wives and husbands are to behave. We stayed up half the night talking over these Scriptures. Marlo asked me to forgive him. I told him some of the things Belinda had taught me. He started to become excited about building a loving relationship with our children and me.

Two months later, my husband gave his life to the Lord. Marlo and I started attending church and going to a weekly Bible study at Belinda and James's house. I joined a women's Bible study group on the base and was astounded at the genuine love the ladies offered.

Gradually, God taught me about forgiveness and being quiet. He gently showed me how to let go of the reins of my life and marriage. Letting go and hanging onto God's hand for strength was extremely hard. But I no longer felt alone because I knew I had Jesus. The darkness and silence that had once enveloped me in fear became a sanctuary where I could sit and pray.

As time passed, God restored our marriage and made it whole. We actually fell in love with one another all over again. But it was a different kind of love. It was stronger and deeper than when we first got married. God even gave us a heart to have more children. As Marlo and I have grown closer to God over the years, we've also grown closer together. It took God's power to clean up the mess in our lives . . . and to make me glad I married that man!

∼ Elizabeth Montes

Finding My Own Faith

"Aw, NOT AGAIN," I whined as I slumped in the back seat of the car. "Why can't he just take the money?"

"Shush!" Mom waved a hand toward me. "Your dad's just helping someone. He doesn't feel right about taking the money."

"But . . ." I started to protest. Dad had just finished talking to the man he'd helped and was now putting a tire jack back into his trunk. We'd already seen the man take out his wallet and try to hand Dad a few bills. Dad refused the money. Instead he shook hands with the guy and headed back to our station wagon.

"We coulda used the money," I sputtered. "We coulda got hamburgers on the way home or something. At least once."

My dad opened the car door and climbed into the wood-paneled station wagon that held his wife and six children. Dad smiled at Mom. I frowned. Far as I could see, the job had been worth at least twenty bucks. That would have gone a long way at the White Castle. We could have bought bunches of tiny burgers for ten cents each. Instead, we drove away empty handed.

That was the story of our family. No money. Lots of good deeds. Dad pastored a small church. Good deeds were practically part of his job description. In between taking the Bible apart during the week and putting all those truths back together for people to understand on Sunday morning, my dad visited people in the hospital, helped couples work out their marriage problems, and listened to troubled teens.

Mom loved the confused and hurt people who came into our lives just as much as Dad did. They both had an incredible faith that was as much a part of their lives as breathing. God was real. He was kind and good and cared about all of us. Knowing this, my parents gave their time, their talents, and the little money they had to help other people find God.

Amid their passion for God, my parents never forgot their six children. We were their first priority and greatest joy. "I don't need money," my Dad would say, "I have six wonderful children." Dad and Mom took us camping, for long hikes in the woods, and spent hours listening to us.

I admired my parents' faith, but I didn't have any reason to seek God myself. He was the center of my parents' life. That was enough for me, because my parents were my life. My perspective began to change at school one day.

"Children, put away your books," my third-grade teacher announced. "We are going to the gym."

I shivered with excitement as I shoved my books into my desk and ran to line up at the door. Our class marched to the gym and sat on the floor. A policeman talked to us. He told us about a very dangerous person who had been stalking children in our neighborhood. At least one child had been abducted and killed. The policeman wanted us to watch a movie that was scary but very important. We watched a re-enactment of a recent abduction. A girl about my age was lured into a car by a strange man. She ran through the woods to try to get away. Then the film drama ended. A few seconds later the screen showed the picture of a child in shorts and a T-shirt, lying in a stream in the woods. Her face was blurred out, but the bruises on her arms and legs revealed that she had been beaten before being murdered.

I closed my eyes, but I couldn't forget what I had seen. As I sat cross-legged on the gymnasium floor, my eyes fastened on the little body that was purposely out of focus, I realized that my parents could not be everywhere. My sense of security weakened. For one horrible moment I had glimpsed a truly flawed world. I worked hard to forget that day, and I stayed closer to my parents than ever before.

"You kids need to help your mom more," my dad said one afternoon after church. The lunch dishes were scattered across the table and there were dirty pans sitting on the stove. In a matter of minutes, my father had organized a cleanup crew. My job was to clean the floor. I waited until the kitchen was clean. After everyone left the room, I started to sweep the floor. The job seemed endless and monotonous.

Swish, swish. Pulling the broom across the worn linoleum almost lulled me to sleep. Finally, I had swept the entire kitchen floor and had a pile of dust and crumbs ready for the dust pan. As I stared at the pile, I noticed the silence. I couldn't hear the screams or squeals of my siblings at play. Someone had turned the radio off. I didn't hear my mother and father talking anywhere in the house. I looked around the kitchen and into the rooms on either side.

"Mom? Dad?" My voice echoed in the emptiness of the house. Where had everybody gone? Without the warmth of family conversation, the walls stood dark and cold. I was alone, completely alone. To this day, I don't remember where the rest of my family had gone. What I do remember is the loneliness I felt that afternoon. For some reason, I felt like the only person in the universe. I did not like that feeling. Without my parents as a barricade against the scary world, I was afraid and I was alone. For the first time in my life, I longed to know God for myself.

"God," I said as I clutched my broom, "please take over my life. Forgive me for my sins and make me clean inside. I'm scared and I want to know you."

In that moment, the God of my parents became my God. His goodness and kindness belonged to me. I could talk to Him every day, and He listened. I was His child. My parents' faith had finally become my own.

As time passed, I even began to understand my dad and mom's good deeds—they were so thankful for what God had done for them that they couldn't help but meet others' needs. As an extension of their love for Christ, they loved others.

And if you look closely, you might even catch me doing good deeds—for the same reason.

~ *Reneé W. Hixson*

Finding Christ at the Carnival

"I LEARNED ABOUT Jesus today," my older sister Carmen declared on the way home from the school we attended that week in yet another small town. We were a carnival family, traveling across Germany from fairground to fairground. I was seven years old.

"Who's Jesus?" I asked.

"He's the Son of God," Carmen said. "He loves everybody, especially children."

"Does He love them even when they are bad?"

"Yes. The teacher said you can go to Jesus with all your problems. He'll always love you and help you."

"Where is Jesus?" Josefa, my younger sister, asked.

"He's in Heaven. You can't see him, but He sees you."

"Then how can you go to Him?" I asked.

"You can pray. You fold your hands, like this." Carmen stopped, shrugged her shoulders to settle her backpack more firmly, and pressed her hands together in front of her chest. "You hold your hands like this, then you thank Him for everything and tell Him all your troubles."

That sounded good to me. I needed someone to talk to, and Jesus seemed like just the right person. I decided I would pray that night in my bed in our cramped caravan home. But by the time we went to bed, I'd already forgotten.

A few weeks later at a different town's fairgrounds, I played between our caravan and the tractor while Father put up the merry-go-round. A local girl approached me.

"Can I climb the tractor?" she asked.

"No. My father doesn't like it when we play on it."

I noticed some papers peeking out of her pocket. I pointed at them. "What are those?"

She pulled them out and showed them to me. "They are about Jesus," she said.

"Jesus," I said. I remembered that I had planned to pray but forgot. I felt vaguely guilty. Then I remembered what my sister had taught me.

"He's in Heaven and loves us," I said.

The girl gave me the pamphlets. "You can have them. I can get more from my church."

I looked them over. They had pictures and didn't seem too hard to read. A kindly looking man with a beard smiled at me from the first page.

"That's Jesus," the girl said.

I thanked her and stuffed the papers into my pocket to read later.

In the evenings, we children usually sat around the kitchen table, playing quietly. If we were quiet, Mother and Father, who read or played chess in the middle compartment of the caravan home, sometimes forgot we weren't in bed yet and let us stay up longer.

After I finished my homework that night, I pulled the pamphlets from my pocket to read them. One told about a girl who was crying because she lost the money her mother had given her to buy bread. The girl remembered that Jesus would help her, so she stood in a corner and prayed. When she looked around after the prayer, she found her money.

I loved that story, and the others like it. At the end of the stories, the pamphlets said to be as good as you could, and Jesus would always love you and protect you. When I went to bed that night, I practiced praying and felt warm and protected.

In the morning, while Mother was spreading margarine on our breakfast rolls, I bowed my head, folded my hands, and started to thank Jesus for the food.

"What are you doing?" Carmen asked.

"I'm praying."

"Praying won't do you any good," Mother said, shaking her head in disapproval. Her dark eyes were hard and cold. "You're so naïve."

I looked down at my roll and suddenly didn't feel like eating it. After that, I didn't pray in public, but I still always prayed quietly in bed.

One night I woke up shaking. I'd had another nightmare. In it I saw dead bodies and skeletons under our caravan home, ready to grasp my ankles and pull me under. I whimpered, not daring to make too much noise, or Mother and Father, who slept on the living-room sofa, might hear me and get mad. Desperately, I folded my hands and asked Jesus to make the skeletons and bad dreams go away. A warm, safe feeling coursed through me. I felt as if a bright, shiny hand was over my head. The power coming from that hand flowed through me from scalp to toes, and a deep peace washed over me. Somehow I knew that Jesus knew me, loved me, and would never leave me.

That summer I attended church in many of the towns we visited. If a church wasn't too far from the fairgrounds, Mother would let me go, just to have me out of the caravan home for a bit. I would ask around at school, and when I found a child who was willing to have me tag along, I'd go with her. I learned about Jesus dying on the cross, and I was glad He loved me and had taken away my sins with His suffering.

The winter when I was sixteen, for the carnival off-season, our caravan returned to Wetzlar, the town where we had wintered for several years.

One drizzly November day, my sisters and I were wandering around the city when we saw an announcement in a store window. "Learn English for free," it said. Underneath it declared, "English classes offered for free by two young men from the United States."

I read the words again. I wanted to learn, wanted to know more than what my grade-school education, by then complete, had given me. English was so popular, and I was tired of the lack of education in my life and the constant travel. I was tired of the never-ending parade of drunken yokels who considered me easy prey because I lived with the carnival, and who so often made my life in the summers unpleasant. Maybe during this winter I could learn something that would somehow change my life.

"Wait," I said as Carmen and Josefa walked away. I fumbled in my purse for a pencil and a slip of paper and scribbled down the address where the meetings would be held.

"It's free," I told them. "Let's go together and learn English."

"Why not?" Carmen said, and Josefa, too, agreed it would be fun.

We walked home, talking about attending English class and impressing the youth in the different towns we would travel to the next summer.

Promptly at 7:00 P.M. the next Wednesday, my sisters and I arrived at the room where these Americans would hold class. Two young men stood by the blackboard, speaking a foreign language. We sat in the back of the room as a few more people drifted in. Three teenage boys sat behind us and whispered to each other.

I watched the Americans. The tall, dark-haired one regarded us with summer-blue eyes. In accented German, he introduced himself as Mr. Ellis. His partner, Mr. Bishop, was shorter with red hair and glasses. He didn't seem to speak much German and was content to let Mr. Ellis introduce him. They handed out pencils and registration forms, and class started. For an hour I listened, spellbound, repeating the strange English sounds and taking notes.

After the lesson, the Americans said they were going to present a short slide show about their church. They said they would appreciate it if we stayed to watch. A young couple rose and left, but the teenagers, two older women, and a man stayed, along with my sisters and me.

What I heard that night changed my life forever. The slide show told the story of a young man who saw God and Jesus in a vision. *Yes,* I thought, *I, too have seen God's hand in a vision. Maybe He has led me here on purpose.*

After the slide show, Carmen pulled on my arm. "Let's go," she said. "I don't want to wait around to be converted."

I wanted to stay, but Josefa had already opened the door, so we left.

All week I thought about the Americans and what I had heard in their slide show. I so wanted to do what was right. *Maybe Jesus sent me to this English class for a reason,* I thought.

I could hardly wait for the next class. That Wednesday, Carmen had lost interest and Josefa couldn't go, so I went back by myself. After class, Mr. Ellis asked me where we lived, because we hadn't written an address on our registration forms. Since it was hard to explain where we lived, I asked them to come with me to our caravan home. I would show them our living quarters, and they could talk to my father.

The two Americans accompanied me through the quaint city, with its crooked streets and tiny stores. Street lamps marked faint circles on the narrow sidewalks here and there. As we walked, Mr. Ellis told me about God's love for everyone and how every person needed to pledge his or her heart and life to the Lord.

When we arrived at my home, my father, always friendly, invited the two in and asked about their country and their families. He even knew an English word or two. But when they started to talk about Jesus and church, Father became irate. He was a "good Catholic" and didn't need any other religion.

Mother stared at the two Americans sitting on the sofa. "There is no God," she said. "Or He wouldn't allow all the misery we went through during the war."

The two Americans tried to explain. Their German wasn't good, and I don't remember exactly what they said. I already knew the war and bad stuff wasn't God's fault. But how could I explain? Mother would get mad if I interrupted. "If your daughter wants, can we tell her more about Jesus?" Mr. Ellis asked Father.

"Yes, if she wants," Father said.

I nodded my head. I wanted them to teach me more, even if my family ridiculed me. I knew there was a Jesus and a Father in Heaven and that they loved me. That seemed so much more important than what my family thought of me.

That night after I said good-bye to the Americans, I fell to my knees behind our caravan and surrendered myself, and my future, to Jesus. That night I also realized that my first commitment was to Him, then to my family. Let them think what they wanted; I was going to do what was right.

The next Sunday I put on my prettiest dress and went to the kitchen for breakfast.

Josefa stared at me. "Sonja wants to go to church," she said, grinning. "What a dummy."

"Just don't get too religious," Mother called from the living room. "You have to live in the world, too."

I sat on the bench and quietly chewed my breakfast roll. The two Americans had invited me to their church, and I was going to attend, no matter what my family said.

All that winter, I regularly attended church. I met people who became my friends, people who believed as I did and helped me learn more about Jesus. I also kept attending the English class, and by the time my family went on the carnival circuit again, I knew the language quite well.

A year later Mother separated from Father, and we moved with her into an apartment. Since we were staying in one place, I attended church regularly—in spite of the teasing I still received from my mother and sisters.

I eagerly studied the Gospel and soon realized that when I followed the Bible, my life was better. In spite of many temptations, I never drank or smoked, and I vowed to God that I would stay a virgin until I married. I kept close to the Lord through daily prayer, and He guided me through the pitfalls of my youth and eventually rewarded me with a wonderful husband. We moved to the United States, where we raised our children in the faith. I can't imagine how different my life and the lives of my children would have turned out, had it not been for the hand of God guiding me from earliest childhood.

Many people seek entertainment at the carnival, but I found the greatest thrill of all: Christ.

～ *Sonja Herbert*

Missing Person—Found by God

MISSING-PERSON NOTICES SEEMED to be posted everywhere in Kansas City. Young prostitutes were disappearing from the streets of the inner city, their bodies found later in the muddy waters of the Missouri River.

While crews dragged the river in search of more victims, I posted a notice of my own. "Have you seen Michelle Steele?" the first line of the notice asked in big, bold letters.

The notice looked like many of the other missing-person notices, but it had one striking difference. The person whose image appeared on it—Michelle Steele—wasn't missing. She had been found more than a year earlier—by God. The story of her conversion to Christianity was printed inside the "missing person" notice, and the back of the notice listed steps that readers could take to give God control of their lives. I know all about this, for I am Michelle Steele.

Before coming to Kansas City, I had lived in Nashville as a drug addict and prostitute. My life started spinning out of control when I was in my teens. Although I was raised in an affluent family, I ran away from home at the age of sixteen and soon became entangled in life on the streets. I met a young man my age who introduced me to prostitution and later married me. We had two children together, but even that did not cause us to come clean. For eight years, we lived immersed in crime and addiction.

Then, with his grandmother's persuasion, my husband went to church one Sunday. He came home wanting to know more about God. Since he couldn't read well, I reluctantly read the Bible to him. I couldn't understand why he now seemed to have more interest in God than drugs. I refused to go to church with him.

Days later, he accidentally overdosed on drugs. The doctors at the hospital told me he was brain dead, but they kept him alive on machines. While I was at his side, a preacher from the church Bo had visited came to see me. He didn't look like any other preacher I had ever seen. He had a long ponytail, a beard, a biker's vest, and a giant Bible.

"Michelle," he said, "do you know how much God loves you? Do you know how much God wants to help you right now? But He needs you to ask Him for help. He wants to put your life back together. God can help you get off drugs. He can help you be the person and the mom you want to be."

I stared at him in disbelief. How could he say that God cared about me when I was at the lowest of lows, with my husband dying in a hospital room? "You don't know who I am," I said. "You don't know the crimes I've committed. You don't know the things I've done."

"That's right," he said. "But God knows, and He loves you anyway." The thought that God might love me was startling. I sure would like for it to be true, I thought. That would change my life.

The preacher asked if he could read a Bible verse to me. He chose Romans 10:9, which says if we confess with our mouths that Jesus is Lord, and believe in our hearts that God raised him from the dead, we would be saved.

I accepted the truth of that verse, and I prayed, "God, I believe in my heart that you died for my sins and that you rose from the dead. I ask you to change me and help me get my life back together. From now on you're in charge of my life."

After the preacher left, I went down to the emergency-room bathroom, removed a packet of cocaine from my shoe, and injected it into my arm. For the first time, the drug had no effect on me. I didn't feel the usual high, and when Bo died shortly after that, the drugs in my system didn't console me.

Over the next two months, I struggled to get off drugs with the help of a government program, but the medications only made me sleepy. I wrecked two cars while on those drugs, and I accidentally overdosed. Both of my children were taken from me. Devastated, I called the preacher who had visited me when Bo was in the hospital, and he and his wife invited me into their home.

The next morning, I went to church with them. Still heavily medicated, I fell asleep during the service. Another preacher at the church woke me and asked, "Do you want help?"

"Yes," I answered, and he prayed for me. For the first time in eight years, I felt sober, and I could think clearly. I made a decision right then to truly know Jesus as Lord and Savior, and I quit taking drugs without any of the sickness that usually comes with trying to quit cold turkey.

Over the next year, I spent every spare evening I had in church. I found a happiness there that I had never experienced before. I felt free. I found a job as a waitress, rented and maintained an apartment, and regained custody of my children. I also met Philip, the son of the preacher who had awakened me and prayed with me, and at the end of the year we married.

Philip took an insurance job in Kansas City, and we moved to a town nearby. When I saw the drug addicts, prostitutes, and homeless people on the streets of Kansas City, I felt a tug at my heart. I knew I needed to help.

So I saturated the inner city with the missing-person notice that asked, "Have you seen Michelle Steele?" I spoke to people on the streets, in rehabilitation centers, and in homeless shelters. Soon, people recognized me, and they told me that learning about the change in my life helped them make changes in their own lives. My husband and I and other members of our church began taking these people to church on Sundays and treating them to a home-cooked meal afterward.

We now bus about 200 adults and children to church every Sunday, serving lunch in the church afterward. On Saturday mornings in the summertime, we go into the inner city, set up a sound system, and play children's music for the kids who live there. We sing songs with them, play games, give out prizes, and tell Bible stories that teach how to make good choices in life. At Christmas, we give out thousands of toys to needy children, and at the beginning of the school year, we distribute thousands of backpacks to kids who can't afford them. Throughout the year, I teach substance-abuse classes and speak in prisons and churches.

I find myself driven to help the downtrodden in society. How can I not? After all, I know what it's like to be lost . . . and to be found.

∼ Michelle Steele, as told to Ronica Stromberg

The Silent Sentinel

As I ENTERED yet another hotel room, the gray tinge of the overcast, damp April day in Michigan matched my mood. At the edge of the motel parking lot was the remnant of a big winter storm—a pile of half-melted snow, now filthy with road grime, waiting to melt away. But I planned to be gone—not just from the motel, but from my troubled life—long before the snow melted.

As a traveling salesman, I had spent twenty years living in one hotel room after another, and they all looked pretty much the same to me. But on this night I'd chosen the motel for somewhat sentimental reasons. Though it wasn't as nice as my usual accommodations, I'd stayed there with my wife many years earlier. Since then, my career had brought fame, riches, and all the trappings of success into my life, far beyond my wildest dreams. I was the envy of my associates and closest friends. In fact, even as I entered the hotel, back in Illinois, my wife and three young adult children were comfortable in a beautiful home, where they owned exotic cars and enjoyed a very expensive roof over their heads.

Unfortunately, behind that façade of success, my life was a different story. I had been living two lives—one at home and one on the road. Drinking had become a major issue for me, and worse, lonely nights on the road had led to one affair after another. As years passed, it only got worse. Eventually my wife and children learned what I had been up to. I was sure my wife would soon leave me for another man. My children had simply turned on me—they hated me.

After checking in at the front desk, I went to my room and called my wife. The conversation with her was cold and bleak, and it confirmed that I'd come to the end of my rope. I was empty, spent, and beaten.

Hours passed, and finally, in that dark room, I decided to call the desk clerk for a middle-of-the-night wake-up call. I thought it would be my last call, as I planned to leave in the middle of the night, get in my car, and run it into an abutment I'd seen up the road from the motel.

When I reached for the phone, something fell from the nightstand onto the floor. I flicked on the light, and saw a Bible at my feet.

Although I didn't know it at the time, this Bible had been placed in my room just a month before by some faithful Gideons. For months they'd prayed every week to get permission to place God's Word in this motel. The motel manager had felt it wasn't a good idea because his motel was near a major university, and the students often partied in those rooms. But the group had continued to pray on their knees, in the hotel's restaurant where they met, faithfully, trustingly, always knowing nothing was impossible for God.

Now this Bible at my feet was open to the first pages, a help section, where references for dealing with despair, loneliness, pain, and many other emotions that I was feeling were listed in black and white. Using the help section, I began to read one verse after another. I just kept reading. Hours passed, and for the first time in weeks, I fell asleep without sobbing. It was a peaceful sleep. When I woke, there next to me on the bed was the Bible, and Christ was in my heart. I rolled out of bed, got to my knees, and prayed a rather simple prayer: "Jesus, please help me."

From that very moment, my twenty-year alcohol dependence was over, and the multiple affairs and addiction to that lifestyle were also over. I propped up the Bible in its place on the nightstand, where it stood as silent as a military sentinel. Yet as I'd experienced the night before, this "Silent Sentinel" was ready to spring into action.

I checked out of the motel and drove back to Illinois with the Lord at my side. He stood with me in the face of one personal tragedy after another: the loss of my job, bankruptcy, divorce, three grown children who hated me, and a world turned upside down. But, you see, when I was at the end of the rope of my life and finally let go, Jesus had caught me with His outstretched arms and His pierced hands.

God's Word is powerful, His grace is beyond our limited wisdom, and His forgiveness is life saving. Years passed, and along the way the Lord provided an angel, a Christian wife to share with me in many ministry commitments. I continued to pray for my children because I had no contact with them. Then one day my daughter visited us and asked if she could be baptized in our church. A few months later she was married there. A couple of years later she asked us to come to her church for our grandson's baptism.

My youngest son, who boldly told me that he didn't love me, now lived thousands of miles away in Hawaii. Again, years passed. During a brief phone call, he asked, "How can you tell a Christian from a non-Christian?"

As a salesman, I had learned to look folks in the eye to detect lies and to see where they were coming from. So I replied, "By the smile in their eyes you will know them." The Bible says you can tell who Christians are by their actions.

One day as my son left his apartment he noticed the older woman across the hallway picking up her paper. She always had a beautiful smile on her face. Her eyes were warm and created a beauty that was kindness itself. He asked her, "Why are you always smiling?"

"I'm a Christian," she simply said.

I had prayed every day for years that God would send a Christian to influence my son in a positive way. Praise the Lord—later my son sought out a church.

My older son was trapped in the foul clutches of heroin addiction. I understand that very few ever crawl out from under that rock. Again, for years, though I had no contact with him, I prayed for him and asked others to pray for him.

Then one day my daughter called. The kids had an unspoken agreement to not talk about each other when they talked to me. But this time my daughter said about her brother, "Dad, he's not a drug addict anymore. He's been drug-free for a few years now."

My daughter waited for a response, but I was too busy sobbing on the other end of the line, tears streaming down my face and joy welling up from within, praising the Lord.

It was just one Bible. But how many people, how many lives were touched?

Years later, I continue to serve my church in various leadership positions, on committees and ministry boards, as a Promise

Keeper volunteer, and as a Gideon. Outside of my home church, as a Christian businessman in the community, I am a Rotarian, diligently adhering to the motto "Service above Self." With the Lord's help, I have worked with other men in my church to form men's ministries at other churches. I've passionately spoken of my relationship with the Lord at worship services in countless churches in Canada and the United States and behind prison bars.

How many people, how many lives, have been and will be touched because of one precious copy of the Word of God—one Silent Sentinel—in a lonely motel room? God answered the faithful prayers of those Gideons to get Bibles placed in that motel just one month before I got there—remarkable! But think about this: more than a billion Bibles have been placed, one at a time, by Gideons around the world. My story is a story about just one.

Some may say this is my personal testimony, but I say it's God's testimony, the testimony of His extreme love for us. I thank God for pastors who recommend men from their churches to become Gideons, and I thank God for Christians who financially support the Gideons. All it takes is one Silent Sentinel to give folks like me, who are out in the traffic lanes of life and might never make it inside a church, the opportunity to read God's Word.

~ David R. Simerson

Learning to Give Up

WHAT HAPPENED TO those first Christians who were willing to die for their faith? No one seems that enthusiastic anymore. The thought struck me one day as I was in church—where I always was on Sunday mornings.

I'm not sure what started the train of thought. Perhaps it was because one by one, the gals in my circle of friends were getting saved and they were excited about it. They started this little prayer group and invited me.

"No way!" I responded. I had five kids. I figured I didn't have time to go to a group where women sat around gossiping.

Finally one day I joined them. What a surprise to find out that they weren't gossiping but praying. They prayed about their families, about church, about others coming to Jesus—they probably even prayed about me when I wasn't around!

But I liked the changes I saw in these friends' lives. One day one of them gave me a book that talked about having a relationship with God, and as easy as that, I asked Him to come into my life. It wasn't because we were having big problems in our family or anything—I just knew a good thing when I saw it.

The day I gave my heart to Jesus, one thing that convinced me of the reality of my new relationship with the Lord was an immediate sense of joy. Nothing I had ever experienced compared with that joyous feeling of total well-being. It was like an artesian well, springing from within. Definitely not something I worked up on my own.

I could hardly wait to tell Jerry, my husband, what had happened. Of course he would be excited for me and want the same thing for himself, I figured. That was my first surprise as a new believer. Apparently I didn't know him as well as I thought, because the moment he walked in the door that evening he sensed a difference in me, and he was not happy. He definitely didn't want any part of it for himself!

As the days passed, he grew even more horrified. My basic interests changed. I didn't want to go out drinking anymore or do some of the other things Jerry and I did. I instantly stopped smoking. I wanted to read the Bible all the time, and I wanted to talk about Jesus and what I was learning about him—but I couldn't do that with Jerry. I got involved in this prayer group and Jerry certainly didn't like that. He seemed to feel threatened by it in some way. Jerry wanted his "old wife" back, but I had become a "new creation," as 2 Corinthians 5:17 describes, and knew I would never be the same. I honestly didn't try to preach to him—well, at least not that first day. But a solid wall sprang up between us, and though we occupied the same house, we were miles apart for the next few years.

One day, about three years later, I relinquished everything that I considered "mine" to the Lord in a deeper way than before. I held it all out for Him to use however He wanted to open Jerry's heart to salvation. I gave God our marriage, family, home, health—my very life. I already knew that everything belonged to Him, but giving it back was a wonderfully freeing experience. The rest of that day I felt lighthearted and refreshed.

For the first time in a long time I was actually eager for Jerry to come home from work. When he arrived, the kids were happy, the house was reasonably clean, a good meal was ready, and his first words to me were, "I've decided I can't live like this anymore. I want a divorce."

What? That wasn't supposed to happen! I gave it to God to *fix* things, not destroy my life. I felt betrayed. Shattered! Eventually I got around to talking to Jesus about the mess He made, and realized that when we give something to Him, He takes us seriously. Even though it's really not ours to give, He accepts our offering, and gets down to business.

I gradually recovered from the initial shock of realizing that the Lord was doing what I asked, without checking with me first to see if I approved of His method. I handed it all to Him. He took what I offered, and the strangest thing happened. In the midst of that terrible tempest, His divine joy began to bubble up in my heart again.

I could even see God's sense of humor as the events of our lives unfolded. Although Jerry said he wanted a divorce, he found excuses not to leave. The funniest was that he was a coach for one of our sons, and he didn't want to move until after football season.

We were both too stubborn to make ourselves uncomfortable, I guess, because we continued to share the same bed. With five children, the only extra sleeping space we had in our house was a couch, and neither of us was willing to go there.

Finally we were down to the wire. He planned to move out the next day, but that night he admitted, "I just can't leave the kids. I want our marriage to be better, and I'm willing to try."

Most people agree that it doesn't work to hold a marriage together just for the children, but in our case, God used Jerry's love for them to keep us from separating. If he had moved out, I doubt that we could have gotten back together.

Throughout this time, the Holy Spirit revealed aspects about my own life that needed to be worked out—some things I didn't necessarily care to know. He began making necessary changes in me and opened my eyes to see Him in our situation.

I learned so much during that trial, including how to trust God, even when things look hopeless. He gave me the grace to love my often-less-than-lovable husband. I'd have preferred just watching everything fall into place like a fairy tale, but God obviously didn't think that was the best plan. He showed me that my job description never did include remaking Jerry into the man I wanted. The Lord made it clear that I needed to concentrate on becoming the person I was created to be, while He worked on my husband.

I devoured Christian books, but quickly discovered that it didn't help to leave any placed around hoping Jerry might read them. He wouldn't. One spring I started reading Chuck Colson's book, *Born Again*, not realizing that Jerry was going through a phase of being fascinated with anything to do with the Watergate mess. The author of that book had been Nixon's advisor and part of the Watergate scenario. He'd come to know Christ in prison, and that's what the book was about. With no devious planning on my part for once, Jerry picked up that book. It's pretty long, but he read it in three evenings. The kids and I saw tears in his eyes occasionally, which he quickly mopped away. He finished the night before Easter.

The next day wasn't very different from any other, except that Jerry did let the kids and me go to church—he didn't always. But that evening as we were getting ready for bed he said, "I think we should start a business."

We had discussed that before. For several years he had wanted to open a restaurant, but I had disagreed. I knew where I'd spend my time, and KP duty didn't sound fun.

But that evening he said, "No, let's open a Christian bookstore."

My first thought was that he wanted to set me up in business so he wouldn't feel bad about walking out on us. The next thought was, *He's crazy!*

"Christian bookstores aren't like other businesses. You have to *be* a Christian to run them," I calmly told him.

His response, "I am," didn't faze me. He always insisted he was a Christian, so that was nothing new. I was a fanatic, in his opinion, but he was a Christian. He went through catechism as a kid, used to go to church (before he got mad at God and me), lived in America, and hadn't murdered anyone. Besides, he wasn't anything else. Must be a Christian.

So I kept arguing. Finally he said, "I've given up fighting."

I still didn't understand what he was saying, until eventually he told me that he'd finally seen God's love and power and realized he really wasn't a Christian. He had given his heart to Jesus on his own.

When I finally stopped arguing and began to pray, I discovered this wasn't Jerry's crazy idea—it was God's. I still wasn't wild about it, but we began planning. Amazing things happened, and it seemed like miracles were sprinkled through the work and plans. We learned about CBA—Christian Booksellers

Association. They have a convention every July, which fit perfectly with our plans to open the store in August. That year the convention was in the city where we lived—that was the *only* year it was ever here.

We discovered the best place to order fixtures and then found out that they always set up a model bookstore at the convention. No one had placed any orders yet, so whatever we wanted would become their model store. After the convention we could take the fixtures directly to our store, thus not paying any freight. And because they were doing it for a trade show, we knew they'd use their very best displays.

The last evening of the convention always features a huge banquet with a big-name speaker. That year it was Chuck Colson! Afterward, Jerry told him that he had given his life to the Lord as a result of reading *Born Again*. Actually, what he said to a gracious Mr. Colson was "I figured if God is powerful enough to change someone as nasty as you, I might as well give up."

I'm so glad Jerry gave up. I'm glad I did, too. When I gave up living on my own, I found a relationship with Christ that will never leave me. And when I gave up on my home and marriage, God stepped in.

∼ Ardy Kolb

Faith in My Sleeve

"IF AT ALL you have become a Christian, do not make public confession, but keep it within your sleeves!" my father rebuked me.

"Today you are spoiled and have become a vagabond," another relative said.

My friends said about me, "He has adopted a foreign religion and left his original one." And one of the religious leaders in my hometown of Udhampur in northern India threatened to kick me all the way to America.

This is how my family and friends responded on the most precious day of my life, the day I received Christian baptism as a symbol that the old Prem Chand had died and the new one had risen to life through Jesus Christ. In my heart, I thanked God for leading me out of a dark religion into the light of Christ.

Born in the state of Jammu and Kashmir, I was taught to worship nature and Hinduism's myriad gods, who are said to be higher than any other gods. Although our family worshiped the monkey god Hanuman, the strongest of the gods, I began to have doubts.

These doubts emerged when, as a teenager, I was unable to live the good life I desired. The harder I tried, the more some other part of me kept gaining control. Ashamed of the way I was living—stealing from my parents, lying, reading bad magazines—I cried to my god for help. But my god did not answer.

Other things bothered me as well. If our gods were so great, why did they not help my father out of alcoholism? Or our family out of its extreme poverty? And why did we all live in such fear of witchcraft and sorcery? What was the benefit of worshiping such gods and goddesses?

In great distress, I visited a famous shrine in our area called Vaishno Devi Katra. To reach it I had to travel thirty miles, ending with an arduous climb by foot into the high reaches of the Tirkuta Hills. Exhausted from my journey, I fell before images of the goddess: a raven-haired woman perched upon a tiger, her many arms jutting from her scarlet robe. As I bowed to pray, I felt a hard slap on my back as the temple priest demanded that I leave. I did not know that I was supposed to have paid a bribe to worship in that place.

Deeply hurt, I returned home more distressed than ever. At times I would look upon the sun, moon, stars, and stones that we worshiped and know in my heart that their beauty must prove the existence of a supreme power who was loving. But who was that supreme power?

At about this time, my uncle Shranku heard the gospel message from American missionaries and turned his heart over to Jesus Christ. Like many Hindus, my uncle had practiced various forms of the occult: spiritism, witchcraft, and sorcery. Such practices had held him in fearsome bondage to dark powers, which he could not break. But when he knelt before the One God and asked Jesus Christ to come into his life, my uncle was filled with such a sense of freedom and joy that he resigned from his job in military service and devoted his life to full-time Christian ministry. Sometimes Uncle would take me with him on evangelistic trips. As we traveled along the dusty roads, he told me what God had done in his life, and he reasoned with me.

"I understand your struggle," he said. "But you have already seen that your gods cannot help you. It does not matter whether you do penance or dip in the River Ganges—these are external acts that will never bring you peace inside."

"Then I am without hope!" I cried.

"No. There is a way. The Bible tells us there is only *one* God, and one mediator between God and men, the man Christ Jesus. Even though this man was God's Son, He died on a cross to pay for all of your sins. Because of this, God can forgive you and give you peace of mind."

"Why would He do that?" I asked.

"Because He is a God of love, not a god of fear," Uncle replied. I pondered his words, wondering if this was the god who had made the lovely things in nature. Soon after, my uncle invited me to attend his church. After the service I asked many questions of the pastor, and when he asked whether I wanted to know Jesus, I could hardly wait to bow my head and ask God to forgive my sins. Then a divine light chased away the heavy darkness inside me, bringing peace beyond human understanding. With joy, I went away praising the Living God.

In the days to come I detested my old ways more than ever, but now I had power through Christ to forsake them. Even my academic life changed. Once a dull student, often truant, I now achieved excellent grades. My teachers were delighted, but when they asked why I had "changed my religion," and I told them about Jesus Christ, I was denied a scholarship and other benefits I would have otherwise received. My new life would not be without cost.

Soon after becoming a Christian, I was baptized and changed my name from Prem Chand Bhula to Prem Chand Daniel. This custom, when a Hindu converts to Christianity and takes a biblical name, opens a door to telling the curious about the Lord. So right from the start, our tradition is—instead of hiding our faith in our sleeves—to find ways to openly tell others about the change in our lives.

After a time, my elder brother, witnessing the good changes in my life, turned his own life over to Christ. He took the name John. John and I prayed for our younger sister, and she, too, turned to the true God. "We must now pray for our parents," we agreed, so we did so and talked with them constantly about Jesus Christ and His salvation.

At first my father insisted that any religion would do, as long as a person lived a good life. But when severe sickness came upon him and my mother, they each tearfully repented of their sins, asked the Lord for new life, were healed, and were baptized into the Christian faith.

Now out of school, I became employed as a civilian in the Indian army. There, I distributed New Testaments, and led two officers to a knowledge of Christ.

Over the next several years I prayed for a Christian wife, and God sent me a woman named Grace. We married and had two sons. We named them Ashish ("Blessing") and Anand ("Joy"). Since my name, Prem, means love, we consider our family titles to be Love, Grace, Blessing, and Joy!

When my boys were young, my vision to share my faith increased. I began to feel heavily burdened for people in the remote Himalayan mountain villages north of us. So my wife and young sons accompanied me on mission journeys. We climbed steep and narrow paths through dense forests where leopards and bears were known to roam so we could share words about Jesus even farther away. Later, my brother and I traveled into the mountains together, walking for ten to twelve hours to bring people the good news about Jesus Christ. Many Hindus, Muslims, and Sikhs who had never heard this message received it with joy.

When my sons were teenagers, my burden for northern India became even greater. I came upon Bible verses such as Isaiah 6:8: "I heard the voice of the Lord, saying, 'Whom shall I send? And who will go for us?' Then I said, 'Here am I. Send me.'" And 2 Kings 7:9, where four lepers said they weren't doing what was right if they kept the good news they'd learned to themselves.

Although I was head clerk in an army installation, I felt urged to leave the security of my government job and enter into full-time service to God. My brother John and I founded a local church so we could better reach the people of Jammu and Kashmir with the gospel. At first, having no building, we worshiped on the open hillsides. But as sister told sister and brother told brother, it seemed no time at all until we grew to a congregation of 300.

Today we not only have our own building, but the number of churches in outlying areas, including Punjab, has grown to twenty. My family members have also been unable to keep their faith in their sleeves. My wife, Grace, along with other pastors' wives, leads women's prayer fellowships. My sons, now grown men, both minister in our Calvary Mission School, which has eighty-five students. And many of the young men who fervently preach the gospel in the mountain regions today are the boys we reached in our earliest evangelistic endeavors.

India faces perilous times. But as we face an uncertain future, the words of the prophet Jeremiah come to me: "Then I said, I will not make mention of him, nor speak any more in his name. But his word was in mine heart as a burning fire shut up in my bones, and I was weary forbearing, and I could not stay" (Jeremiah 20:9). I am so thankful my uncle did not hide his faith. And as we face the future, my faith will also remain out of my sleeves.

~ *Prem Chand Daniel, as told to Karen Strand*

The F.A.T. Girl in the Mirror

"YEAH, YOU'RE GOING to be a model, all right," the boys at school teased, "a model for *MAD* magazine."

My face turned bright red and I bit my lips—I wished I'd never told them that I wanted to be a model someday. And I was glad I hadn't told them my full desires. Not only did I want to be a model, I wanted to be a supermodel. I connected with models and celebrities because they represented perfection to me.

Unfortunately, no one ever used the word "pretty" to describe me. In fact, my nickname was "Bozo." My mirror clearly told me, "You're ugly. You're fat."

So I began to become obsessed about my appearance.

I never did make it to supermodel status, or even model status, but as I grew up, my life was still all about "the outside." I really believed that physical beauty would bring me satisfaction and recognition. I bought all the false promises: *If I'm beautiful, I will be happy and successful. I'll be desirable to men, and I'll feel secure, important, significant, and confident.*

I worshiped the god of beauty, youth, and self. Since my self-esteem and self-image were tied to my physical appearance, inevitably I felt worthless and humiliated because I couldn't measure up to the standards I was trying to attain. *The prettier, the thinner—the better,* I figured. So I started to do anything

I could to get thinner. I exercised obsessively and abused diet pills, diuretics, and laxatives. When I heard that smoking cigarettes could suppress your appetite, I became a chain smoker.

The more attention I paid to the outside, the less I paid to the mess on the inside. On the surface, I appeared to be a woman "dressed for success." I looked and played the part of a competent marketing representative. No one would have suspected my secret life of misery and feeling horrible about myself.

By day I was Ms. Jekyll, a good businesswoman. But at night I morphed into Monster Hyde. No matter what my weight was, when I looked into my mirror at home, I was fat and unattractive. But I was also starved. So Monster Hyde went into an uncontrollable feeding frenzy. Then guilt and anguish—and the fears of fatness—struck as soon as the food passed my lips. Like a junkie taking a hit of heroin, I got my food fix, followed by a gruesome episode of self-induced vomiting, and then a smoke. That cigarette would burn my freshly irritated throat, but it would suppress my appetite. Bulimia became my daily ritual of weight control.

I also drank and partied a lot as I tried to gain control over my life. I liked getting drunk because then, with my reserves down and my senses blocked, I could forget I felt like an ugly loser who hated herself. I could be someone else, perhaps that supermodel.

Following each binge-purge cycle or drunken episode, I was struck with intense guilt and fear. Then, of course I was overwhelmed with feelings of shame, remorse, self-hatred, and worthlessness, because logically I knew bulimia and drunkenness wouldn't turn me into who I wanted to be. I'd swear to myself, *This is the last time.* But it never was. I needed help!

I was too ashamed to ask for help, so I tried to heal myself by reading self-help books until my head was about to explode. Because I was a marketing representative for a hospital, I knew a lot about certain medical protocols, and I carefully followed the advice given to patients with addiction. But that didn't work. Nothing worked. My life was filled with lies, secrecy, isolation, and shame. It was a picture of bondage, and I couldn't take living that way anymore. *Help me!* my soul cried.

What I needed was someone to point me to God, and God sent that person. A friend asked me to go to church with him. Although I'd gone to Sunday school as a kid, church never had much of an impact on me. When I went to church with my friend, for the first time I heard about the "Good News" that Christians always talk about. I started to listen and digest new truths. The pastor of the church said, "God loves you and wants to enter a personal and intimate relationship with you. He has a special plan for your life."

I thought, me? The loser? He doesn't care that I'm ugly and fat?

I wanted to hear more.

The pastor quoted 1 John 4:10 in the Bible, saying that God showed us how much He loved us by sending His only Son into this world to bring us eternal life through His death.

The pastor said that Jesus' life makes a relationship with God possible.

Wow! A relationship with God! I knew this was the life I wanted. I wanted a life that revolved around being accepted for who I was and how I looked—not the important celebrity model I knew in my soul I'd never be. I wanted a life that was free from the oppression of food and substances. Here was my chance to start all over, fresh and new. I wouldn't be turned away or rejected since I learned that God cares about our hearts, not what's on the outside. That resonated with me. With prayer I invited Jesus Christ to come into my life through the Holy Spirit. It was that easy!

Then God did something miraculous—He took away the *physical* urge to binge and purge. But I was a new Christian and didn't see God's hand in this. I would never have thought myself worthy of a miracle—after all, miracles were for people who had more faith in God and themselves than I had, for people who were able to believe that they were special.

So instead of seeing my lack of desire to binge and purge as a gift that God had given me and a work that He had done, I thought God had merely helped me finally get control over my life. I went on with my life, never letting anyone in on this secret. And I went to church *almost* every Sunday, but I kept my Christianity as a Sunday thing. I didn't give my mind and soul daily spiritual nourishment of reading my Bible, praying, and learning more about this God who loved me no matter what I looked like.

Since I didn't have the desire to obsessively eat and purge, I began to drink alcohol nonstop. I began to have problems with my stomach and ended up seeking medical help. I asked God for healing, and again He came to my rescue. As I worked through my illness, He took away my desire to drink every day. Again, I went on with my life, not wanting anyone to know I'd had this addiction and therefore not admitting to anyone what God had done.

A few years later, I found myself unemployed and in that dark place again. I turned to God, and this time I really felt God calling me into a relationship with Him. I learned that I needed to stop trying to be in control of my life—including my obsession with looking good and being impressive.

Instead, I needed to give God control over my life. *But if He's in control, I can't make the decisions. I have to follow what He guides me to do,* I realized. That was difficult because I didn't know what He had in store for me—*He may ask something of me that is too difficult or uncomfortable,* I worried.

It boiled down to trust. If I gave my life to God, could I trust Him to take care of me? As I began to delve into the Bible and prayed, and checked out other resources, like Christian radio and television programs, I realized that God had my concerns and interests at heart. Whatever He asked me to do, well, He knew what was best for me. And since He loved me relentlessly, He wouldn't do anything that would hurt or destroy me.

Walking the path God blazes takes a huge act of faith. My newfound faith told me that He'd show me the way. I could see now that although I'd accepted Jesus as my Savior years before, I had not surrendered my life to Him. Surrender—relinquishing control. Yes, this is what I had to do.

I prayed. "Father, I thought I could do everything, but now I see I can't do anything by myself. I've been beat up, knocked down, broken to pieces. What do I do now? Will you pick up the pieces? I surrender. I'm defeated. I'm ready for you to direct me and mold me into the person You want me to be. Restore me, please. I see that it is You who can give me strength to fight—only You. I am weak, Father. I'm confessing to You now. I want You to take over my life. Amen."

For the first time, I surrendered my heart, soul, and will to God. One of the first steps of faith I took was admitting to my needs, telling my story in front of the congregation at my church. I got baptized to symbolize that my old life was gone and that I was walking into a new life with God.

Instead of being in control and thinking that God was just helping me, I finally understood *and really believed* that apart from God, I could do nothing. I committed to start reading the Bible and to start talking, or praying, to God every day—as well as turning to Him many times during the day. That was the genuine start of my relationship with Him.

Now God could work on me and with me. Together, God and I started on an incredible journey to clean up the *emotional* garbage—the self-esteem issues and longing for importance—that had led to my destructive behavior and addictions. It was a process. My heart and soul were wrapped with layers of stuff—years of rejection and hurt. I had to let God peel away each layer and fill me with His love and guidance. I had to let Him take my past, my life, from the dark to the light.

When I brought my issues into the light, the healing began, and I eventually was set free from my past. With that freedom came peace and inner quietness because the struggle was over. I was securely in God's hands. I didn't need to turn to food or booze or pills to find peace. Once I surrendered to God, peace flooded my soul. God restored me to the person He created me to be—spiritually, physically, emotionally, and relationally. I lost my life, only to find it again. My nightmare turned into a dream.

And then God connected me to women who had been in like situations, who had felt similar pain. We became "Jesus with skin on" to each other, which fostered healing and change in our lives. I felt free to talk about my past. I leaned on Jesus to give me the compassion and counsel to help others and show women like me—who felt ugly and rejected—how to see themselves through God's eyes. As I became God-centered and began to reach out, I found a security growing within me, and my focus changed from myself to others. The same comfort and love I receive from God enables me to help others. And that has been the key to my ongoing transformation into Jesus' image. God has blessed me with empathy for women in pain, and today I am a graduate seminary student with several outreach ministry projects.

Now when I look in the mirror, instead of fat and ugly, I look to see a different kind of "f-a-t"—"faithful and true" to my Lord!

~ Kimberly Davidson

The Measure of a Man

"You've got to smell like a man!" These are some of the few words my father ever spoke to me. He grew up on the wrong side of the tracks, in a Kansas railroad town where he learned to swear, smoke, and drink. This was his idea of what a man should be. Men should smell like sweat, tobacco, and whisky. He was a tall, stout man, all muscle, and strong on discipline.

He only had to speak once, and I'd answer, "Yes, sir!" No telling what would have happened if I'd given him any lip.

Dad slept with a pistol hidden under his mattress until the day he died. I remember, as a kid, taking it out and playing with it one day when I was alone in the house. It's a wonder I didn't kill myself or one of my four siblings, because it was loaded and didn't have a safety.

All of us kids knew we were to be "seen and not heard." We were always well fed and clothed, but we never heard the words "I love you" or much other conversation directed to us. Instead, our home was filled with yelling and my mother's screams. I recall leaving the house one time when my parents were quarrelling, intending not to return, but I was only eleven years old, too young to make it on my own.

My fraternal twin brother, Darold, and I were not alike by any stretch of the imagination: he was tall; I was short.

I struggled with school, flunking the third grade. Darold was quick in his studies, and eventually graduated magna cum laude, with a doctorate at the age of twenty-five.

Darold was already two grades ahead of me when we got to high school. No one ever pushed me to do my homework, so I didn't do it. Showing up in class every day became more painful as the years progressed. One time, I came home with a bad report card, and Dad said, "You're just like me, barely getting by."

Well, if it's good enough for Dad, it's good enough for me, I thought.

My father was a pioneer union railroad man—his only identity. But when he went on strike against the railroad, he lost his job. We moved to Fort Worth, Texas, where he was hired at General American Tank Corporation and promoted to superintendent. Eventually he lost that job and had to go on unemployment.

Many years later, Darold and I discussed the circumstances that eventually caused our father to question his conclusion about what made a man, an awakening that would influence his family.

I told Darold, "Losing that job was the best thing that ever happened to him and our whole family. Because he was at the end of his rope, he started to look for answers."

We all found those answers in a little church not far from our house, the Sagamore Hill Baptist Church. One day, a lady from church came to visit our home and invited us to attend Sunday school. My mother, who had a Baptist background, encouraged us children to go.

The pastor was great with kids. We loved him because he played ball with us. This influenced Donald, our older brother. Jesus didn't enter our family with the blare of trumpets and the pounding of drums. He slipped in through Donald's heart. Donald wasn't too fond of his little brothers and sisters tagging along with him to church, but he put up with it.

One night during a revival, an evangelist preached a stirring sermon while our parents were there. I was about thirteen years old, sitting in the front row, swinging my feet back and forth since I was so short. Out of the corner of my eye, I saw my forty-five-year-old father stepping down the aisle, taking the preacher's hand. I didn't have any idea what was going on that night, but I was soon touched by the change in my dad. *Surely, there is something to this man they call Jesus if He can change someone like my dad!* Beer vanished from our refrigerator; fights and yelling flew out the door. What a change! My home was as different as night from day.

Out of work and still on unemployment, my folks decided to move back to Kansas. There, my brothers and I worked for a dairy farmer, hoeing corn. Dad also worked full-time for him, barely earning a living wage. My folks borrowed money on their house and bought a small dairy. With five children to bottle milk and make deliveries, we made it through some tough times.

Jesus edged His way, little by little, in among us. Some church family friends, the Adduddells, suffered a devastating loss when their daughter, son, and an uncle were all killed by a train that broadsided them while they were returning from the son's graduation from Oklahoma Baptist University.

They will quit going to church because God has let them down, I reasoned.

After the funeral, however, they came to church and worshiped God. I saw something in them I wanted and needed. Mrs. Adduddell was one of our customers. I'd take her milk to her house and then I'd sit with her in the living room. I could talk with her. She became a mother figure and my spiritual mentor.

I decided to follow Jesus, saying, "Jesus, be my Lord, because I want You to tell me what to do with my life." I asked Him to be my Lord long before I realized He was my Savior. That sounds odd, but that's the way it was. It wasn't until later I came to understand what Jesus did for me—taking my sins on the cross where He died for me.

A few years later, my world turned upside down again. I'd volunteered for the draft at eighteen, and as soon as I got home, my wife, Lila, and I had our first baby boy and went to church every Sunday.

"Harold, I want you to preach." Every Sunday, I heard God's voice whisper over and over again. Surely not! I find it difficult to read, and anybody who's flunked a grade can't be prepared for the ministry.

"Harold, I want you to preach."

I cried every time I heard a sermon. Life was upsetting, because of His voice speaking to me, and urging me into another way of life. Finally, only when I said, "Lord, I'll try to do what You're calling me to do," did I find any rest.

We had three children by this time, and I had a good job working for the Missouri Pacific Railroad. I decided to go to the community college so I could keep my job. I was not prepared for the visit from Mr. and Mrs. Adduddell.

"Harold, why don't you go to Oklahoma Baptist University?" they asked.

"There's no way we can do that."

Later, Lila said, "Why can't we go to OBU?"

We found out that this was the last year I was eligible for the GI Bill. Lila and I decided we could do it. When we told our parents, my dad said, "You'll be back in six months." Lila's father said, "You're taking my grandchildren down there to starve to death."

My sister was the only family member who supported us in this decision and helped us move. But with government aid, lots of prayers, and by the grace of Almighty God, I graduated.

My mother couldn't believe I earned an A in Greek and made the Dean's Honor Roll. She carried that report in her purse until it wore out. At her urging, I'd gone to high school one hour a day to finish and get my diploma. No wonder she was ecstatic I'd gone to college and graduated. To both of us, it was unbelievable after the years I'd spent struggling in school.

My speech teacher told me, "Harold, when you were accepted on a trial basis to OBU, I never thought you'd make it, but you did."

I spent years preaching the gospel of Jesus Christ, and now have four grown children and twelve grandchildren who serve the Lord. I trust that my eleven great-grandchildren will be doing the same.

My life has been good. I learned a long time ago that a man isn't measured by the way he smells, or how tall he is, but by the size of his heart and mind's commitment to serve the Lord and others.

~ *Harold E. Morgan*

When Excelling Isn't Enough

THE FATE OF the entire Korean race in America depended on me.

Or that's the way I was raised to feel, anyway. Like most Korean immigrants who moved to the United States in the 1970s, my parents were graduates of top universities who left white-collar jobs in Korea to start over from the bottom in America. They hoped the successes of the next generation—my generation—would justify their sacrifices.

I was the firstborn of four siblings. We grew up in a Buddhist family headed by my perfectionist father, described as the Asian Captain Von Trapp—a reference to an unbelievably strict father in pop culture at the time. My tough-as-nails grandmother made herself our live-in teacher. And my creative mother, in her powerless position, told us we kids were all that mattered to her. We all lived in a big house with an impeccable yard in the suburbs of Orange County, California.

As I tried to fit in as an American, I carried the weight of my father's expectations to be a good example, to bring honor to the family—yea, to the entire Korean race. With perfect report cards and stacks of certificates, I had learned to perform. I was captain of the math team, the school's spelling-bee champ, soloist in the honors chorus, and winner of various art competitions.

No one, no teacher, no neighbor could have guessed that I went to bed crying and spent hours pondering how I might end my own life.

Even as a young girl, I was aware of the discrepancy between the hurting, struggling, real me, and the picture-perfect model minority child others perceived. I knew I was far from perfect. My life was a farce, like an act in which I must don heavy armor to hide the truth of a home life full of marital turmoil, incredible stress, and occasional violence. I was torn between what I felt was my responsibility to protect my mother and my younger siblings and my desire to escape from the unbearable burdens placed on me.

Since I was hopelessly depressed, thoughts about death—a way out of the pain—consumed me. I'd study kitchen knives to see which one would do the job most painlessly or stare into the medicine cabinet. On one desperate occasion, I ran out of the house to just get away, but my grandmother found me sobbing and scolded me for making my parents' troubles worse with my tears. I was convinced that I did not matter to my grandmother, that I would never be good enough for my dad, and that I could not go on being my mom's confidante. Feeling like a thirty-year-old in a child's body, I didn't fit in with my peers at school and spent my free time alone—thinking, wondering, searching for a purpose for my existence, for some redemptive reason to persevere. I distracted myself with music and even an imaginary friend, but they could only momentarily drown out my feelings of being unwanted, inadequate, ugly, and rejected.

In middle school, I thought I'd found my place in a group of friends whose childhoods—having been disrupted by divorce, molestation, rape—left them with deeper things to talk about than the latest brand of jeans. And with my first boyfriend, I so desperately wanted to believe that his "I love you's" were true. I could not even consider the possibility that a hormone-driven, smoking, drinking, spiritually lost boy would not be capable of fulfilling his promises. I learned little from our breakup and slavishly craved male attention, which I generously received because I sought it so much.

One day, I was on the phone with a guy when my father, stretched to breaking point from a string of business failures, burst into a rage. The next thing I knew, I was knocked over and my dad was holding the phone handle with the disconnected cord dangling in his white-knuckled fist.

The next day at school I showed up with a wide black circle on my eye. When I thought of my father, my heart screamed, "I hate you!" But I still tried to protect him when I was asked what had happened. I told everyone I had accidentally been struck by a ball.

Before half of that day was over, I was unexpectedly called into the principal's office. There, I was shocked to see my parents. My mother sat puffy-eyed and with her head down, and my father sat quiet and strained as he was informed that he had earned a child-abuse record. For a man brought up in the old Confucian ways of discipline and scholarship—always respected for his intellect and his stature—this was an unspeakable humiliation.

Years later, I would find out that shortly after this event, he drove himself to a church parking lot where he bitterly wept. All I knew was that one Sunday morning, in his typical authoritarian fashion, he ordered us to get dressed. We were going to church—a Protestant church!

For weeks, I reluctantly assented to losing my Sunday mornings. Toting my teen magazines, I sat in the back of the auditorium and pouted. For too long, my job had been to keep up appearances, and I was sick of it. Angry and bitter, I trusted no one. But my mind was increasingly curious, and my heart was starving for something more, something beyond, something bigger than the dark hole that I felt was my existence. I so desperately wanted something to prove that my life was not futile after all.

As words began to seep into my mind through the barricades I'd tried to put up, I wondered, could what the preacher was saying be true? Or is God something like Santa or the Tooth Fairy, created by adults to keep their children in line?

If there was a God, I wondered, was He truly good and all-powerful? Could He be trusted? Did He truly love me? I listened. I wrestled.

I didn't know anything about Christian literature, so I looked up entries about Jesus Christ in every encyclopedia set I could find in my high school library. Then, I began to read the Bible for myself, starting with Genesis.

Finally, on Christmas Eve that year, restless and unable to sleep, I dropped to my knees by my bed. With urgent whispers, I cried out in the darkness, "God, are You there? I'm so tired of living . . . I've made such a mess of my life . . . Are You for real? Or am I just talking to this wall? Oh God, I really need You!"

At that moment, I sensed a Presence in my room. I sensed that He was so awesome and holy that I was keenly aware of my own unworthiness and uncleanness. And yet, I was strangely comforted. Like water bursting through a broken dam, the tears flowed freely. And God received them all.

After some time, I was overcome with peace. I got up and tiptoed into the living room where I reached for a hymnal my father had recently purchased. I didn't know any sacred music, but I sat before the lit Christmas tree and flipped through the pages anyway—my heart wanted to sing! My thumb stopped and I recognized the words: "Silent night, holy night, all is calm, all is bright."

I had sung these words many times before for holiday programs at school, but for the first time, I understood that God had sent His Son as a baby in a manger to be the Savior of the world. And on this Christmas night, He had entered my room, my heart, to rescue me! The love my heart was aching for could never be satisfied by human relationships. Neither could my search for meaning be answered by more achievements. But the Savior of Christmas had perfect love to make me secure at last.

I could not have imagined then how far God's healing would go in my life. As I grew older, a fear of marriage—or more accurately of being locked into an empty or abusive relationship—kept me wary of men. What's more, I could not fathom being a mother. Who would want to bring children into this broken world, anyway? But as I recognized that my life was not my own, that it rightly belonged to the loving God who made me, I found my fears overcome by faith and hope.

I have now been married for fourteen years to my true love and am honored to be called Mommy by six beautiful children. As for my relationship with my birth family, on my twenty-seventh birthday, my father mailed me a card filled with tender words of affection and regret—he asked me to forgive him for that black eye. Asian culture does not require an elder to apologize to a child, and he had never done it before, so this was real evidence to me that the Holy Spirit was working in his heart. Sometime after, he was ordained as a minister in the Presbyterian Church, with my mother serving beside him.

My siblings have all been touched by the life-transforming power of Jesus Christ, too. My sister serves as a nurse in a Christian medical outreach program in Chicago, and my youngest brother is a career missionary in Japan. Perhaps most amazing of all, my grandmother, a devout Buddhist of seventy years, was almost unrecognizably changed by God into a loving, gracious woman. She battled with cancer for a year after her conversion and then went home to her Savior.

So much has changed. Still, every Christmas Eve, I sit before the glowing Christmas tree and recount how the One called the Light of the World came to grant a suicidal teenage girl trapped in darkness and death a purpose and joy for life.

～ Caroline Seunghee Roberts

From the Good Life to a Better Life

CAN YOU IMAGINE spending more money on dry-cleaning your suits than most people bring home in a weekly paycheck? Imagine ordering take-out from the finest five-star restaurants in town, just because you felt like picking at a little something to eat while you sat in your townhouse watching your big-screen television. Imagine taking a cruise to the Caribbean, then doing it all over again just a few months later, just because you could.

By the time I was in my thirties, I was doing that and more. I had lived hard and fast for most of my life, and climbed the corporate ladder. When I reached the top, however, I found the view wasn't as attractive as I had expected. I became bored with it.

I don't remember much of that life now.

When I was just forty-one years old, an aneurysm ruptured in my brain and I suffered a major stroke. My perfect life shattered as quickly as a porcelain figurine crashing on a concrete block. The splintered fragments of what was left of my past self could never be glued together again, and I would never be the same. Everyone, including me, began to pray to God for a miracle. The only thing was that I didn't know how to pray. I didn't know what to pray because I never knew Jesus.

After undergoing brain surgery, I spent six and a half weeks recovering in intensive care. The days blurred together as therapists and nurses worked with my body to rekindle some semblance of my former self. I had to learn to talk in sentences again, although I often repeated myself and gurgled when I spoke. When I was finally released to continue recovery at home, I remember sitting on the porch and asking Jesus why this was happening to me. Me, the one who always had her life under control. The one who always took care of everything by herself, for herself. I had never needed anyone or anything from anyone else because I basically got everything that I ever wanted, when I wanted it. I certainly didn't want to have to deal with this new affliction, pain and suffering.

My mother had told me that when all else fails, pray to the God of the universe. I realized I desperately needed real help from a real God. And so I asked for it. I prayed for forgiveness and for strength. Although I doubted that He would hear me, I prayed to Jesus to come into my life, make me whole, and open my eyes to a new world. I vowed to accept whatever as long as He would be with me through it. Amazingly, not only did He hear my prayer, but He also answered it beyond my greatest expectations.

The odds of surviving a ruptured brain aneurysm are not good. The odds of thriving after one are even worse. My medical prognosis held little hope for me to return to the workplace as a productive member of society. I only needed to look at the many whose lives had been devastated by strokes to understand the cruelty and consequences of traumatic brain injury.

Then came a miracle, another answer to prayer. Against all odds, I returned to work eight months after the catastrophic brain hemorrhage. But within a week of my return, God made it clear that He didn't want me to be there. My job might have been high powered, but He had more for me than the good life I'd been living. About this time, a friend of mine called to tell me about a fairly new business enterprise called Curves for Women. Less than two weeks later, my sister and I traveled to the Curves corporate headquarters to make a deposit on our own fitness franchise.

Two months later, in December of 2000, we opened our Curves franchise in the Hudson Valley of New York. Now I jump all day long at our Curves, mostly for joy. I have no doubt that this is exactly what I was saved to be doing at this moment in time, for I have an incredible opportunity to minister to women of all different backgrounds. I was saved to serve them.

A few memories of my past life do remain, like the day that I asked for forgiveness from Jesus—I will never forget that moment in my life. But most of the memories have been erased by the brain trauma. I have short-term memory deficits, but I surprisingly can remember the name and something important about each of our Curves members. I know it is a gift from my Jesus.

When I am asked today how I feel about my ordeal, I answer, "It was a blessing in disguise." I have found a common thread in folks who recover from a near-death experience: We are grateful for the chance to do it right the next time around.

I believe I was so hard-headed that God had to use an aneurysm to get my attention and draw me to him. He knew it would take more than a gentle nudging by the Holy Spirit to unlock my potential to enter a relationship with the King of Kings. And it took a miracle afterward—the miracle of recovering with such slim chances—to convince me that I am royalty, the daughter of a King. I am worthy of a better life—an eternal life.

~ Michele Starkey

Set Free

SIRENS SPLIT THE night sky and, as usual, the spinning lights were coming for me. I pulled over for the same old routine, but this time, I panicked. I was already wanted in another city.

I am not going to jail! I decided. So as the cop approached the car, I slammed into gear and shot into traffic like a crazy bat from hell. In only moments, the streets were chaos as more cops joined our high-speed chase. I'd started the chase, but I was scared to death as I ran cars off the road, zoomed through stoplights, and careened off curbs. My adrenaline was pumping so hard and my heart was pounding so fast that I could barely breathe. I was lucky I didn't kill someone, including myself.

Finally I decided to bail. When I turned a corner, I opened the car door and flew out. A tuck and roll later I was up and running. But I'd obviously seen too many cop shows. My car crashed into someone's house, and I was captured within minutes. I'd been in trouble many times in my life, but this was definitely the worst. I couldn't even begin to believe what I'd done.

Some kids just become bad news at an early age. I was raised in church but got in with some bad kids during elementary school.

I started smoking marijuana when I was ten years old, and drinking at age fourteen. By sixteen, I was addicted to alcohol, and when I was twenty-eight, my first marriage ended because of drugs and alcohol.

After that, I lost all semblance of being clean and sober. I'd get drunker than drunk and do crazy things, like driving as fast as I could on my way home from the bar. Then I got into more serious trouble with the law. I got a DUI. I sold my house and spent all the profit on cocaine and women within two months. I was caught driving without a license two or three times. Then I got another DUI.

The system kept giving me chances. They even put me through alcohol classes. After those classes, however, the students would just walk across the street to the bar. I eventually spent a month in jail, which started to get my attention. But I still wasn't ready to change. I got out of jail, got in trouble again, and went back in. I went through just about every recovery program the county offered. Then I was given "habitual offender" status, which meant the next time I got into trouble, it would be considered a felony.

One morning my ex-wife called me at work to tell me our daughter was sick at school. I borrowed a car and headed for the school, but I didn't slow down for road construction. I got busted. It was a God move, although I didn't realize it at the time.

So I got my first felony, but I thought, *I can beat this. I'll just get a good lawyer.* I spent $3,000 on a lawyer, and he did get me a good deal. The judge gave me another month in jail and a year's intensive probation, which meant I had to check in all the time, go to classes twice a week, take drug tests, and be constantly monitored. I attended the classes and quit drugs for a while, but I soon started using again.

Still thinking I could beat the system, I drank goldenseal and other herbal teas, which I'd heard could give clean results on the drug tests. I even drank vinegar, thinking I was fooling the system, thinking I was so cool. I did six tests with no apparent problem. After the seventh test, the teacher said, "I need to talk with you after class."

As cool as I could be, I said, "What's up?"

The teacher didn't miss a beat. "Your first six tests were hot for THC and marijuana, and this last one for THC and cocaine. I'm going to have to drop you from the program and make a motion to revoke your probation."

I'm not going to prison! I thought. So I ran to another town, where I hid out at a friend's place. I didn't want to be found by the authorities, or my ex-wife for that matter. After all, I didn't pay child support, either. I was a deadbeat dad. I was a deadbeat everything.

I worked for several months for the friend I was staying with. He also sold drugs on the side, so I'd work all week for him and still end up owing him money for my usage. It was awful. At times my heart pounded so hard from the cocaine that I thought I was having a heart attack. I'd pray, "God, please. If you're really there, you need to help me, because I can't help myself."

Then came the apex of my trouble—the night of the police chase. I'd been driving to another guy's house to pick up an ounce of cocaine when I noticed the dash lights go out in the car, which meant the taillights were also out. That's why the cop had pulled me over—to let me know my taillights were out. And that's why I ran—because I knew if he looked up my record, I was going to jail anyway.

A week after the chase, I was released on bond. Feeling at the end of my rope, I returned to work and waited to go to court. I was shocked when the pastor from the church I grew up in showed up at my hideout. I was petrified that someone had found me, but I was glad to see him. He told me the Lord had sent him to me. Then he asked if I wanted Christ in my life. I said I did. He prayed with me, and God's Holy Spirit just knocked me down. I sobbed and sobbed.

The system gave me yet another chance. This time, they put me into a community corrections program. I spent four months in jail waiting to get a bed in the halfway house. Finally I went through the halfway house program with flying colors. I had no write-ups and was out in record time. I was able to stay away from drugs when I got out, but Satan knew my other weakness—women. He put one in my life who professed to be a Christian, although she smoked pot and drank a lot. I was around the booze and the pot for months without any problems. Then we started having troubles in our relationship. On top of that, I saw my ex-wife and my kids during the holidays. That was too painful for me. One night after Christmas, I got loaded—drank myself into a blackout and drove without a license.

When I woke up the next morning, I was in my own bed but coated with blood. I figured I must have gotten into a fight and didn't remember it. When I looked out the window, I couldn't see my car, so I went around the neighborhood and found it several blocks away. I called my case manager.

Because it was a Saturday, I left a message on his machine saying I had used again, and I was scared.

"I want to take care of this," I told him. "I want help."

A week or so later, he contacted me and told me to turn myself in to the halfway house, which I did. I thought they would send me to a treatment program, like they had countless other people. But instead they told me, "We've revoked you from our program."

"You're not going to send me to treatment?" I said.

"Sure we are—prison. You'll learn there."

I didn't understand how this could happen. "That's what I get for being honest," I told the jail chaplain. "I should have lied, never said anything. They would have never known."

"But you know what happened, and God knows what happened," the chaplain pointed out. "God also knows where your heart is—it belongs to Him now. He loves you, even though you messed up again, and He's going to be with you through whatever comes. You did the right thing by turning yourself in, and God sees that. He's going to take care of you."

I knew the chaplain was right, and suddenly I felt at peace with the whole situation. A little later my ex-wife brought my oldest daughter to see me at the jail before I went to prison. I was smiling. She said, "Dad, why are you so happy? You're in jail!"

"I'm freer now than I've ever been in my life," I told her. "I might be behind bars, but I'm free."

Soon I was sent to prison. When a person first shows up in prison, standard procedure is to keep him locked down for twenty-three hours a day. I was allowed out for one hour to take a shower and use a telephone. In my cell, I exercised and I had a Bible with me that I read and read and read. The isolation was hard, but it was good for me. It gave me time to think and study the Bible. It also gave me time to build my new relationship with Christ.

At first, Scripture confused me. I didn't understand it. The Bible seemed to contradict itself. I asked God, "Please show me something in here that's from you to me." I asked Him for wisdom and understanding and to open my eyes to His Word. As the effect of twenty years of drugs and alcohol left my body, I started comprehending the words and concepts in the Bible, and I began to notice my surroundings. I saw God at work, even in prison.

I asked God to let me be a light to the men around me. Then the blessings began to happen. Guys started saying, "Man, I'm having problems. Can you pray for me?"

I carried my Bible everywhere I went. More than once I heard, "There goes a Bible thumper." But I also heard, "Look at him. He's getting God while he's in prison. You watch him when he gets out."

I attended Bible studies and church groups in the prison. There's no barrier between colors and races in those groups— we're all God's children. I caught a lot of slack if I ate lunch with a black man or a Mexican. The bikers and the white supremacists would try to hassle me, try to break me, verbally and physically.

A couple of times I could have been in a physical confrontation, but the Lord gave me the words to say: "Hey, God loves you, man. He loves you, and I want to talk to you about him." And my attackers would take off. They couldn't handle it.

"Thanks, Lord!" I'd say.

After I was released from prison, I lived with my parents and rode my bike more than thirty miles to and from work every day. After several weeks of commuting by bicycle, I said,

"Lord, you've got to open doors for me. I need a place to live closer to work." I had looked all over for an apartment, and I was getting frustrated.

One day as I got on my bike after work, I looked across the street and saw some apartments with a sign reading, "Faith Property Management." It was like God was saying, "Have faith. Wait on me." I called the number on the sign and moved in two days later.

Now I'm off parole. God has brought a wonderful Christian wife into my life, and He has provided me with a nice home and a good job. People still ask me how I got a house with my bad credit. I tell them, "There's no way I could have done it. The glory goes to God. He gets the praise and glory for everything good in my life."

I am slowly but surely beginning to give back—to society and to God. I've been approved to go into the jail as a religious volunteer, and I'll soon be allowed to go into the prisons. I love going to minister at the jail because I am blessed so much. I'm anxious to get back into a prison, too. I want to show those guys what I've learned: "Hey, God loves all of us."

Maybe I can influence some people others can't. I've got a record. I've got the tattoos. I've done it all. I'm here to say God was gracious enough to reach down and grab hold of me, because He loves me, and He has a purpose for me. He has a purpose for everybody. We just need to let Him show us what it is. And when we find His purpose, we can be truly set free— from whatever prisons bind us.

~ *Gary Carlson, as told to Becky Lyles*

Hopeless to Hopeful

HOUR UPON HOUR, I spent dreaming. I planned every little detail and imagined the people's reactions. I wanted them to react. You see, I was spending all that time planning my suicide. And I fully wanted everyone to know just how unhappy I was. I wanted them to react to my death strongly.

I was twenty-nine years old, and it wasn't like suicide was a new concept for me. My family had moved a lot when I was growing up, so I didn't make good, lasting friendships. To complicate my self-esteem matters, I was a poor student and felt I never met my parents' expectations. I became progressively unhappy and rebellious.

That's part of the reason I married at nineteen. I believed that moving away from my parents would solve all of my problems. Six months later I had my first baby. I knew I would be a great mother because I would do everything opposite from what my mother had done. Fourteen months later, my second child was born. My husband was working long hours and studying for his master's degree. Loneliness crept back into my life.

Soon, babies three and four came along. My husband often worked late, and I resented his long absences. Feeling trapped at home with four small children, I soon realized I was treating my children the way my mother had treated me—with anger and high expectations. I also used foul language and delved into pornography and immorality.

When my husband lost his job, we started a business venture with my parents. Bad idea. Emotionally, that set me right back into the vortex of unresolved issues I'd always had with them. Financially, the venture failed, so now, on top of everything else, we had no job and no money. Anger and depression now permeated my life.

My misery reached a climax when I had extensive oral surgery. After the procedure, the dentist sent me home with pain medication and tranquilizers. My emotional pain intensified my physical pain, so I started taking the pills every hour, around the clock. After twenty-four hours, I had overdosed. I was hallucinating and hysterical.

The drugs wore off, but they'd set alarms ringing. I felt like I was facing a showdown: I either had to change my life or follow through with my plans for suicide.

Desperate and afraid, I agreed to attend when a friend invited us to a church cantata for Palm Sunday. Our family arrived late and squabbling, but when I began listening to the music, God touched my heart. Before long, tears rolled down my cheeks as my unhappiness overwhelmed me.

After the cantata the pastor spoke about sin and love and invited us to give our lives to Christ. As we sang the invitational hymn, I wanted so much to run down the aisle and tell the pastor how I felt, but I was too embarrassed. So I just stayed in my seat and cried.

The next week we returned to the church for Easter services. The pastor preached on John 3:16, talking about how Jesus loved us so much He gave His life for us to save us from our sin. Again he extended an invitation to come forward and accept Christ. Again I felt a strong urge to run down the aisle, and again I stayed in my seat and cried. That week, two ladies from the church visited me at home. They explained how I could give my heart to Jesus and accept His forgiveness and salvation.

Could happiness be that simple? I wondered. I thought of all the things I had done in my life to try to make myself happy, and now these women were telling me that it was a gift from God. I couldn't believe it. But I wanted to believe it. I needed to believe it. So, with tears streaming down my face, I fell to my knees in the middle of my living room and gave my miserable life to Christ.

Though my husband hadn't yet made his own decision for Christ, he was drawn by the gospel, and we began attending church regularly. I couldn't really believe Jesus would come into my heart after one simple prayer, so every time the pastor extended an invitation, I prayed again, "Jesus, if you haven't come into my heart yet, please come now."

A couple of weeks later I saw the lady who had led me in the sinner's prayer. She said, "Diana, I can tell you're a new creature in Christ. I see it in your eyes." Finally, I recognized the peace that God had put into my heart and realized I was saved.

Some things changed immediately. I no longer thought about suicide or used foul language. I lost all desire for immoral behavior and pornography. Other things took longer. It was several years before the relationship with my parents was healed, and I still had to deal with the consequences of my previous sins. But facing problems with God in my life and with His peace in my spirit made all the difference.

Growing in Christ has been an exciting experience. Falling in love with the Word of God, experiencing the intimacy of prayer, sitting under the anointed teaching of pastors and Bible teachers, and enjoying the fellowship of Christian friends have all made my walk with Christ a wonderful adventure. No matter how difficult my circumstances, God helps me through. Nothing can compare with the hopelessness I felt before Jesus came into my life. Nothing could make me want to go back.

$\sim$ *Diana Lee*

Belonging to the Lord

AFTER THE EXAM, my gynecologist announced that I might be pregnant—maybe our plans to have a child had finally been successful! I rushed home to tell my husband the good news. He was eager to share it with the world, but I told him, "No, let's wait. I want to be sure."

A couple of weeks later we discovered that I was not pregnant. Instead, the medication I was taking for ovarian cysts had caused the mistake. It wasn't the end of the world. We were both in our early twenties, so we had plenty of time to have children.

"Do you think our child will have black hair like daddy's, or blond, like mommy's?" "Blue eyes or brown?" These were just some of the questions we asked each other during our frequent conversations about the children we'd someday have.

But a few years later, those children still hadn't materialized. We decided to pursue infertility tests. During one test, a special dye was injected into me to clear any possible scar tissue. I endured painful cramping, but I knew it would be worth it. The nurse assured me, "Many people are able to become pregnant after this procedure."

Another test was extremely painful, and I couldn't hide the agony. The doctor glared at me. "Do you want to have a baby?"

"Yes!" I cried. "You've already started the procedure. Finish it!" In the waiting room, my husband heard me scream.

"It's not worth it," my husband said later as he held me. "We can adopt."

"We can?" I asked weakly. This was the assurance I needed to hear. I felt I had somehow failed him by being unable to bear his child.

Still, we completed all the basic infertility tests, tried fertility medicine, even attempted artificial insemination, all to no avail. The doctors could find no logical reason for the infertility. I wondered if God didn't think I was worthy of being a mother.

Baby strollers littered the world around me. How I longed to hold my own child in my arms! I seemed to spot pregnant women everywhere. I couldn't handle attending baby showers. Friends were reluctant to share their good news with me when they conceived. My husband comforted me at night when I cried myself to sleep. Our dream was shattered in a million pieces.

One day I was scanning our local newspaper when I noticed an ad for an adoption meeting. I realized that I had been so consumed with becoming pregnant that I'd missed the entire point. I wanted to be a mama, not necessarily be pregnant. Surely adoption was the answer to our nearly forgotten dreams.

In July 1999 we received the call. "Mrs. Kim? We've received a referral for you. It's a boy." As the woman at the agency explained the details, tears spilled down my cheeks. I couldn't control them, nor did I want to. Our dreams of parenthood were becoming reality!

Our adoption referral package arrived the next day. My hands trembled as I opened our mailbox, where a large envelope waited. I grabbed it. My stomach fluttered. As I shuffled through all the papers, my heart nearly stopped—there was his picture. He was sleeping with his tiny hands curled up next to his shoulders. His mouth was slightly open. One foot was raised a little, the other flat. Perfect. Beautiful. Our son.

His Korean last name was Kim—the same as ours! Now our conversation was filled with new questions. "What should we name our son?" We finally settled on Dominic.

A month later we received a second phone call, telling us Dominic was to arrive on September 7, 1999. He would be four months old. The day finally arrived, and we waited anxiously at the airport. "Your baby's on that plane," the adoption coordinator explained, "but it will be a little while before they bring him out to us."

After about thirty minutes, the escort approached us and handed a crying Dominic to me.

"Let's try Daddy," I said. As my husband wrapped his arms around the baby, the crying stopped, and Dominic fell asleep. We placed him in the stroller, and our protective instincts instantly kicked in. The airport suddenly seemed much too noisy. Daddy gently lifted Dominic in his arms and placed him in the car seat.

I heard my husband say something, but with all the noise I couldn't understand him. "What?" I asked.

"I'm talking to Dominic," he replied.

He's a daddy! We're a family. Then my mother jitters began. How would I know when to feed Dominic, and how much? How often should I change him? Did we buy the right kind of bottles and formula? Did it matter which diapers we selected? How many blankets did he need at night? I didn't want him to be too cold or too hot.

I dreaded returning to work, but friends recommended a Christian child care that was part of a small church. I decided we should attend a few services to see how they operated and what they believed.

As we walked into the small church for a Sunday visit, people welcomed us warmly. But I wasn't there to be sucked into the church. I was there for one purpose: My son was going to be enrolled in the child-care center, and I wanted to hear exactly what he would be taught.

The pastor spoke of love. He said it was the greatest commandment God has given us. I had to admit that these people showed love, but it couldn't be real. No one could be that nice. *What did they want from me?* I wondered.

A few months passed, and the Bible verses I heard at that church began to make sense. God tugged at my heart. I was invited to attend a women's Bible study group led by a woman named Mrs. Williams. At the first study session, I sat silently as the women around the table shared their thoughts. Did I dare speak my innermost fear? As my heart palpitated and my stomach turned, I finally said, "I don't know how to pray."

As if God himself were answering me, Mrs. Williams said, "He just wants to hear your voice."

God? He wants to hear my voice? Too simple. There had to be more than that. But what did I have to lose? I prayed. I didn't understand, but I gave my heart to Jesus. Two months later, I was baptized. A couple of days after my baptism, I finally understood. God heard my prayer. His love surrounded me in the most intimate and powerful way.

The concept of having a relationship with Jesus became real. Jesus changed my mind, heart, and soul from the inside out. I went from listening to Janet Jackson and Madonna to Michael W. Smith and Jars of Clay. I didn't want to read secular novels any longer, and I canceled my subscriptions to trashy women's magazines. My favorite sitcom of all time, *Friends*, was no longer funny to me. My desire to own an expensive ring to wear on each finger seemed ridiculous. Now I have a cross that I wear, and I never remove it. Without it, I feel naked.

Ironically, Jesus became naked so that I could be clothed. I am now clothed with humility and the desire to become Christlike. I store up my treasures in Heaven, and I long to see Jesus face to face one day.

The biggest miracle Jesus performed in my life was teaching me that my infertility was not to punish me for wrong things I'd done; it was to fulfill a greater purpose. Dominic was meant for our family. Our Dominic has dark brown eyes and black hair like his daddy, and he has a smile like his mommy. Whenever I look into his eyes, I see that he was worth the wait.

When I looked up Dominic's name in the baby names book to find its meaning, it was no surprise to me that Dominic means "belonging to the Lord." Without our infertility, I may never have learned what it means to belong to the Lord.

$\sim$ *Mara Kim*

A Whisper in the Silence

MY COMING TO know Jesus Christ as Savior was not a dramatic Damascus Road event. If anything, it was just the opposite. Unlike the Apostle Paul, I experienced no blinding light, thundering voice, or residual blindness. Instead, I heard only silence and basked in the awesome power of the Holy Spirit's still, small voice.

Because I grew up in a Christian home, my faith pilgrimage was to some extent a process of osmosis. I soaked up the disciplines of Bible study and prayer from my father, who knew the benefits of both, and I saw the effect of his life lived out in faith. From earliest memories, I saw my father's steady trust in Jesus and heard stories of God's faithfulness. One of my fondest memories is of my father seated at the breakfast table, hands folded and head bowed in prayer over his open Bible. He modeled God's character with his life.

While my mother demonstrated her faith a little less, I knew by her love and fierce loyalty to family and church that she believed in God. Her example of servanthood, faithful prayer, and deep concern for others served as a role model for me. Yet accepting Christ had to be my decision—not my parents' decision for me.

Church attendance and involvement were automatic in our family. We never had a question about whether or not we'd be going to church on Sunday. So when word came that our church's sanctuary had been destroyed by a fire, the news was traumatic, like the death of a beloved friend.

During the rebuilding years that followed, we worshiped in a junior high school auditorium, then in our church dining hall. The building process seemed interminable, and we saw only an occasional glimpse of the sanctuary under construction, through parted plastic sheets or partially opened doors.

Finally, the long-anticipated day arrived when we would see the new sanctuary. As we waited outside, I knew it was a momentous day. At last, after the regular morning worship service in another building, we entered the new sanctuary for a prayer of dedication.

I stepped through the door and was overwhelmed by a sense of reverent awe as I viewed the beauty and grandeur of our new house of worship. Sunlight streamed through stained-glass windows, casting rainbow prisms across the floor. Ranks of polished wooden pews welcomed us. Gleaming chandeliers sparkled overhead. This was God's house, and we were invited to meet with and worship Him here.

Everyone else must have been as overwhelmed as I was because a hushed silence filled the room. But in that silence, I very clearly heard the Holy Spirit's voice speak directly to me, "Today is your day of salvation."

As we sat in the center section of the sanctuary, our pastor prepared to offer a prayer of dedication. He bowed his head, then paused. When he spoke, it was not a prayer. "Even though I've already extended an invitation to salvation in our regular service, I feel compelled to extend the invitation again. Someone is here, at this time and in this place, who needs to make a decision for Christ."

I knew I was that person. I looked at my mother and said, "He's talking to me!"

She responded, "Then you must go."

The usual organ music was absent. No choir led a hymn of decision. A flutter of fear filled the pit of my nine-year-old stomach, because as I stood and moved down the aisle, all eyes turned toward me in amazement. This was not the way things were normally done. But the assurance of having heard God's call propelled me forward, and the warmth of the pastor's smile and the touch of his hand welcomed my decision in that unconventional situation.

That day is etched in my memory. The Holy Spirit spoke to me in the stillness, and I've never once doubted that I heard him. I didn't plan, nor was I coached by my parents, to be the first to make a profession of faith in that new sanctuary, but I'm thankful I heard the Spirit's voice, and I'm thankful the pastor obeyed the Spirit by offering a second invitation.

Since that day, many times in my life I've felt far from God and unable to hear His voice. During the early years of my marriage, when infertility sent me into a wasteland of doubt, I wondered if God really loved me and if I'd ever hear His voice again. When my father was diagnosed with cancer and wasted away before my eyes, I wondered how this could be part of God's plan. When my husband lost vision in one eye and nearly died because of complications from diabetes, I wondered if God still walked by my side.

But on innumerable times I've also felt God's presence and counsel, as real as any human friend and advocate—at moments I've felt God providing me with the words to speak during difficult conversations or while sharing my faith journey with those who were seeking spiritually. God faithfully supplies me with wisdom for parenting and marital challenges. He convicts and instructs me regarding attitudes and actions that are not in line with His teachings. The whisper of the Holy Spirit nudges me to change direction when my path strays away from becoming conformed to Christ's image.

Looking back on the quiet circumstances of my salvation experience, I've sometime felt it lacked power because of its simplicity. Surely tales of drug abuse and prodigal-son-like wanderings, followed by fiery conversions, are more dynamic. But over the years God has shown me that He doesn't have to yell to be heard, and He has given me many opportunities to share the story of my coming to know Him.

Several years ago, our church dedicated a new youth building to the Lord. I was asked to share my testimony on an opening-day video. My final words were, "My greatest prayer for this facility is that hundreds of teens will be drawn here by the programs and activities, but that ultimately, they will discover relationships—the greatest being a saving relationship with Jesus Christ. I have a special place in my heart for the first person who accepts Christ as savior in this new building."

Every salvation experience is unique and special. Whether dramatic and thunderous or the result of a whisper in the silence, the Holy Spirit draws the seeking to a saving knowledge of Christ as Savior and Lord. For me, salvation came in the quiet stillness, with a whisper, and that same whisper directs my path today.

~ *Candy Arrington*

The High That Lasts

DOWNING THE LAST of a bottle of whiskey, I surveyed the bedroom littered with empty liquor bottles and beer cans, drug paraphernalia, porn magazines, and heaps of dirty laundry. *What a mess. Just like my life,* I thought. It seemed my life had always been a mess. I'd been expelled from boarding schools, fathered a child out of wedlock, failed in two marriages, and even messed up my army career. *Well, getting high on coke should make me feel better,* I decided. It was 3:00 A.M. when I crashed. Hitting rock bottom, I bellowed, "I hate my wretched life!" Gazing into a wall mirror, I saw the reflection of a gaunt, disheveled, bloodshot, and scraggly-haired thirty-seven-year-old loser. I looked across the bedroom and eyed a loaded rifle propped up in the corner. It beckoned to me so I staggered to it, picked up the weapon and prayed, "God, please take me home."

I awkwardly aimed the rifle into my stomach, squeezed the trigger, and fired. The sound of the gunshot reverberated in my ears, and heat ripped my abdomen.

I woke up in agonizing pain. *Where am I?* I wondered. Looking around, I realized that I was in intensive care. Intravenous tubes snaked across my bed, and a heart monitor tracked my vital signs. Just then, a nurse strode to my bed. Peering at me intently, she gasped. "Mr. Stout, are you awake?"

I moaned in pain. The nurse left and quickly returned with a doctor. "Mr. Stout, how are you feeling?" he asked.

"I could be better," I murmured.

"I'm not surprised. You've been in a coma for the past two and a half months. We'd given up on you. This is a miracle!"

The second miracle occurred two months later, when I was discharged from the hospital with a hip replacement and the extensive damage to my intestines and leg muscles repaired. This brush with death should have served as my wake-up call. It didn't. Convalescing in my parents' home, I returned to my addictions. I thought I was going crazy when, through a drug-induced haze, I began hearing voices in my head. I gradually realized that God was speaking to me. After years of depraved living, He was finally getting my attention. All my life I had dismissed Him as a myth, in spite of my Christian upbringing.

"Batt, you've gotta turn away from your wicked lifestyle. You need to give up the drugs, alcohol, sex, and pornography," God admonished.

"I don't want to," I retorted. Seeking to appease God in other ways, I began reading my Bible and listening to Christian radio programs. However, God grew increasingly insistent that I repent of my sinful lifestyle. While I was lusting over a porn magazine sometime later, several photos began taking on demonic features in my brain. Chills shot up my spine, and my heartbeat quickened. Clearly God was warning me as to the evil nature of pornography. "You've made your point, Lord! I'll toss out my magazines right away," I promised.

Next, God convicted me about my drug use. I told God I couldn't find drug use prohibited in the Bible. God countered my excuses through Scripture verses that labeled narcotics as a form of idolatry. Although my drug use had tapered off, I still got high occasionally. After one such incident, I felt as if God's Spirit was saying, "I'm done with you. You've had your last chance."

"Oh, God, don't leave me! I need you! Lord, please forgive me and cleanse me," I begged, falling to my knees. "I repent of my addictions. Jesus, thank you for dying on the cross for my sins. Now take control of my life, I pray. Please change my heart and transform my life."

This was a pivotal spiritual moment. For the next several months, I studied my Bible day and night. I was a man starving for spiritual nourishment. To my amazement, my cravings for sex, drugs, and pornography evaporated.

On a clear, crisp December morning, I was baptized in my parents' church. As I stood before the congregation, my heart raced with excitement. I confessed my faith in Jesus Christ and received baptism. My heart leapt for joy and my eyes filled with tears. After the service, family and friends congratulated me. But the words my mom said remain emblazoned on my heart. Hugging me, she gushed, "Your dad and I are so proud of you! The whole church has been praying for your salvation for years. Today God answered our prayers!"

This was just the beginning of God's good work in my life. I currently direct the youth group, teach Bible studies, lead a prayer group, and attend Bible college.

But what pleases me most is how thrilled I am to serve God and to spend time with Him. In my old life, only being high on drugs could get me this excited. Serving God is a high that surpasses anything else, and it is a high that lasts.

~ *Batt Stout, as told to Sue Foster*

Never Good Enough

"ALL GOOD PEOPLE go to heaven," I confidently told my friend as we stood talking at a high school retreat. "God is a God of love, so there must not be a hell. A loving God wouldn't send anyone to a place like that."

When I was growing up, my parents took my siblings and me to Sunday school and church. We participated in the choir and other church activities. I studied my lessons and probably knew as much about the Bible and Jesus as most kids my age, but I did not really know the Jesus of the Bible. Instead, I focused on whether or not people acted in ways that were good or bad.

Throughout my early years and into high school, I was usually an obedient, kind, and helpful person—just the sort of person I knew went to heaven. When I moved on to college, I can't say that I stuck with all my self-imposed rules for living a good life. However, I found a church just off campus where every sermon seemed to speak about God's love, and how that loving God was preparing heaven for all those who served Him. That was me. I was kind to old ladies, honored my parents, and didn't steal or kill. So even though my behavior wasn't always circumspect, I figured that I did much more good than bad and relied on that loving God to pave my way to heaven. My eternity was secure—or so I thought.

The week I graduated from college, I married my husband, Hall, and we moved to a tiny town. We joined the only church and started helping there almost immediately. Our first job was teaching teenagers. That was no fun and I felt it was a duty to perform. But since I always had been all about doing what was right, I slogged along with the job I was given.

After our daughter Holley was born, we carried her right to church with us to do whatever duties we were performing. I worked with the vacation Bible school, taught various classes, and did other good works. Though I still did not enjoy the tasks, I knew I was working my way into heaven.

Our second child, Lara, was born eighteen months after Holley. Lara was born healthy and whole, but after her birth, my uterus ruptured. My life was spared, but I couldn't have any more children, and that distressed me tremendously.

I soon plunged back into my everyday activities. In my concept, God was always loving and kind to those who were good. I had been a good wife, a good mother, a volunteer at church, and a helper of other people. Why was I being punished by not being allowed to have more children? Wasn't I good enough? What was good enough for God?

A few months later, an evangelist came to our area. Hall and I went to hear him on the first night of the crusade. As I watched, Hall went forward at decision time, declaring that he had not been a Christian all this time and that he needed Jesus to be his Savior. That was a surprise to me, because Hall was a good man and worked harder for God than almost anyone else I knew.

Early the next morning, Hall left for his annual National Guard training session. I didn't plan to go back to the crusade, but all day a feeling intensified within me that I had to go. I secured places for the girls to stay, wondering, Why do I need to go so badly? I know about Jesus. I'm living a good life. What more is there?

That night, the evangelist talked not just about God, but about Jesus. He said that Jesus was God's Son, that He had come to earth as a human baby and died on a cross as payment for our sins. Now He lived in the hearts of those people who accepted the gift of His sacrifice for our sins.

Mesmerized, I leaned forward in my seat to catch the next words: "You can never be good enough on your own to enter heaven." God seemed to say, "Judy, stop trying to be good. Accept the goodness of my Son; He is all you need."

After the meeting, I bolted from my seat and ran down to the floor, where I was surprised to see the same counselor who had met with Hall the night before. Revelation 3:20 quotes Jesus as saying that he stands at the door of our hearts and knocks. He promises that if we will open the door, he will come in and live within us and be our companion.

For twenty-four years, Jesus had been knocking at my heart's door. He had been waiting patiently for me to hear Him and open the door. That night, not only did I hear, but I threw the door open wide and invited Him in to stay.

After that night, my motive for serving in the church changed. Instead of trying to do enough good works to get into heaven, I do good works because God loves me, and I desire to return that love by being obedient to His leading.

I know that regardless of what I do, I will never be good enough to enter heaven, but that's okay—I know the One who is.

∽ *Judy Burford*

Looking for My Father

BROWSING THROUGH A large department store one day, I heard appeals over the public address system that described a lost little girl. When I noticed a child in the toy section who matched the description, I approached her and asked, "Are you lost?"

"No," she replied innocently. "I just can't find my father."

I could identify with that little girl. As a child growing up in a non-Christian home, I didn't really feel lost. I just hadn't found my Father, God. But I knew He was out there somewhere. I was intrigued by all aspects of nature and often wandered about the huge tree-lined yard of our family farm. Gradually I came to the conclusion that if a carpenter built our house, and my mother sewed my clothes, and a toy maker constructed my wagon, then a mysterious Someone must have made the trees and the river and the fields and everything in them.

My sister was given a Bible storybook, and when I learned how to read, the book taught me this Someone's name was God. After that, I knew it was God who nodded to me from the shadows where the wild violets bloomed. He laughed in the full, rich notes of a robin's song. He chided like a red squirrel, hovered like a mother hen, whispered like the wind.

But sometimes He shouted from the thunderheads and wept in the rain. It bothered me to picture God crying. *Maybe He thinks I am lost.* I wanted so much to find Him and say, "Here I am!" but I didn't know how to go about it. Instead, God kept searching for me by sending other people to help me find my way.

My older cousin was privileged enough to go to Sunday school. She went to one of those churches that passed out Sunday school take-home papers—little leaflets that had stories, scriptures, and games focused on Bible stories and Scriptures. Every week she saved those papers for me. I tied them together with old shoelaces, hugging those Bible stories to my soul, reading them over and over again. I learned a little more about this God I sought.

Kindly Christian women in the community went out of their way to commend me for being "such a good little girl." I realized that people who found God generally knew how to behave themselves, and if these women who I thought knew God approved of my life, I must be on the right track. So with their reassuring words, the ladies kept me from going too far astray.

In fifth grade, we had a new teacher who read portions of the Bible to us. She handled the book tenderly, as if she owed her very life to what it said. Since I knew the Bible was God's book, I watched her life in my quest to find God. In June she presented each of us with a Gideon New Testament. I read it off and on during the next few years, but God was still more real to me in nature than in His Word. I took long walks by myself, meandering along to nowhere in particular, just searching for God. I knew He was out there somewhere, but *where*? The years passed, and I still didn't find the answers.

On the first day of high school, I had another new, young teacher. He quietly informed us that Scripture reading was beneficial for each of us, including himself. As the months went by and I observed his character and lifestyle, I could not dispute that he had an assurance that told me he had found God. Nor could I deny that I was falling in love with him.

Just puppy love, I told myself. Don't get the idea that the feelings are mutual. When the school year ends, he'll find a girl his own age, and forget he ever knew you.

But I was wrong. The feelings *were* mutual. He literally waited for me to grow up and then we started dating. One moonlit night, he stopped the car, took me in his arms, and asked that all-important question: "Do you believe in God?"

The moon was peering down at us intently, as if waiting to witness my answer. Sensing that my entire future hinged on my reply, I took a while before answering. "Yes, I believe in God," I said. "I just can't seem to find Him."

As my relationship with Leo deepened, I discovered God had sent him into my life for more reasons than one. Throughout our ensuing courtship, Leo patiently answered my questions, and I had plenty: Why did God seem so far away? How could I find Him? Was He looking for me too? With each answer, Leo guided me closer to finding the God I sought.

I started attending church with Leo and began to read my New Testament more systematically. I learned that God and I were actually searching for each other, He as a loving Father and I as a lost soul. We were separated by a vast chasm called sin, until God took the initiative and sent His Son, Jesus, to bridge the gap. Bit by bit, with faltering steps of faith, I gradually crossed over that bridge, leaving behind a life of doubt and embracing a new life of trust in God. Compared to those who become Christians in one decisive moment, with one giant leap of faith, the final leg of my pilgrimage to find God lasted for four years and was exceedingly slow, but my arrival was just as certain. God and I had found each other at last, and all because of His Son.

To be lost and then to be found gave me an immense sense of spiritual relief. I felt indebted to God as the Friend I could never repay; it is a lifelong gratitude, similar to the kind someone who has been physically lost feels toward the one who rescued her. Compared to the uncertainty of the past, my future was full of promises—God's promises. Instead of wandering through life with no sense of direction, I now had purpose. God had a plan for me, and with His help, I was eager to try and fulfill it.

The day Leo and I were married, the minister chose Luke 24:15 as our wedding text: "And it came to pass that while they communed together and reasoned, Jesus himself drew near, and went with them." We will soon celebrate fifty years of marriage. While "communing together and reasoning" along the road of matrimony, I have found Jesus to be with us every step of the way. He has given courage when the road seemed all uphill, joy when we reached the mountaintops, comfort in the valley of shadows, and perseverance along the tedious parts of the journey. He has picked us up when we've fallen down, steadied us when we've stumbled, and strengthened us when we've grown tired. He was never out of our sight, and I've never felt lost again.

When I look back now, I can hardly recognize myself as that lost, lonely little girl who once wandered about in the midst of God's creation, searching for her heavenly Father. I still see God's workmanship in a flower. I feel His touch in a feather. I sense His stability in a rock, His power in a wave; they are all manifestations of His workmanship.

I am grateful for the people God sent to cross my path, for they were all signposts illustrating His love, extending their concern, slowly but surely guiding me to Him. What I treasure most, however, is the compass of His Word, which contains a verse that was so true in my life: "And ye shall seek me, and find me, when ye shall search for me with all your heart. And I will be found of you, saith the Lord" (Jeremiah 29:13–14).

∼ Alma Barkman

Righteous for the Right Reasons

My father's polygamy is part of what led me to Christ.

As a boy, I found life very trying because I missed the support and guidance of my parents, especially my father. My father had three wives. He often lived away from my mother, his first wife, and spent the time with his other two wives. I was mainly raised and supported by my elder brother and sister. I missed not having that parental support, and eventually that played a part in my coming to Christ.

My friends and I did attend church. Even though I didn't have as much parental influence as I would have liked, unlike most of my friends I never drank or smoke. I was just what people could call an innocent young man. Despite our church attendance, neither my friends nor I had a personal relationship with Jesus Christ. It was something we didn't even realize at the time.

Becoming a believer was not a spontaneous experience for me. Rather, it was a process that involved some soul searching. It all began in my secondary-school days. I belonged to the usual school clubs, like the Debate Club and the Chess Club. There was another kind of club I could have joined: the interdenominational Christian organization for Christian students, called SCOM (short for Students' Christian Organization of Malawi, where I was schooled). But I wasn't a member of SCOM, nor did I intend to join it. Instead, three of my friends and I liked to poke fun at its members. Sometimes we went to SCOM prayer meetings just to laugh at their way of praying and preaching.

Besides the little group I spent time with, other crazier students attended the prayer meetings to deride the faithful. One of them was a boy named Gideon. During the SCOM prayers, Gideon would roll on the floor and shout "Jesus, Jesus, touch me!" beating his chest as he did so.

But he had nothing to do with Jesus. The aim was to cause fun, and indeed this sparked unholy laughter from non-SCOM members, including me. None of us realized that one day, Gideon would cry those words seriously and end up becoming an Assemblies of God church minister in Malawi.

We did not only mock and laugh at the SCOM members during such prayers. If we saw a pair of SCOM members chatting, especially if it was a boy and a girl, we concluded that they were in an illicit love relationship, and that they only pretended they were believers.

Despite my sometimes-bad behavior, I have an ability to easily interact with people from different walks of life. So although I enjoyed scorning the SCOM members, sometimes I broke away from my friends and had face-to-face conversations with them, especially a young woman we fondly called Agrey. Agrey was not only respected, she was beautiful as well. Interestingly, she did not have a boyfriend at the school, something very uncommon with beautiful girls in my school days. Her singleness made me so curious that I decided to find out why she was not interested in boys.

"I can't accept any love proposal from boys at present because I do not have any plans for marriage," she said.

According to her, girls and boys sinned against God if they engaged in sexual activities outside marriage. Since she didn't want to be tempted to sin in this manner, as so many young people did, she had decided not to date at that point.

Here I was learning a different perception about love relationships from a young woman who feared God. On my part, I did not have a girlfriend, but that had nothing to do with wanting to live a holy life.

Then I asked her what it meant to be a born-again Christian. Her explanation emphasized asking God to forgive your sins such as premarital sex and the abuse of alcohol and drugs and starting a new life by believing in Jesus Christ as "Your Lord and Savior."

Of course, I thought this gospel was irrelevant to me because I regarded myself a righteous person. I did not practice any of the immorality she mentioned.

"What if one is a good person, and does not engage in immorality, do you think God would send such a person to hell?"

On this note, she cited what today I know is Romans 3:23: "for all have sinned and fall short of the glory of God."

The scripture challenged my self-righteousness. Little did I know that all our righteous acts are like "filthy rags" before God, according to Isaiah 64:6.

Although I did not make up my mind to accept Jesus Christ as my Savior, I believe this marked the turning point in my life. It is my feeling that there are many people who are reluctant to accept Christ because they think they are righteous, just as I used to be. Agrey went on to paraphrase Romans 6:23, especially the part that says "but the gift of God is eternal life through Christ Jesus our Lord."

The message of salvation was clear. Though Agrey had already laid a foundation upon which I could build my Christian life, still I did not give my life to Jesus Christ.

It was after I completed my secondary-school education that I especially started to miss the support of my parents. I found myself turning more and more to God for support. I finally succumbed to the tug of God at my heart at a Christian fellowship meeting six months later. I can't remember the exact day or the message the man of God preached. But when the preacher asked those who wanted to start a new life in Christ Jesus to walk to the front, I was among them.

My friends were genuinely surprised when they found I had given my life to Jesus. "But Willie, you don't drink, you don't smoke. So what do you mean you are now born again?" they questioned. But even if it meant they would make fun of me, as we did with those SCOM members, my commitment to Jesus was immediately strong.

Since then, my spiritual life has grown from strength to strength and I now look to my future full of hope. I go to a church where I serve as a teacher of God's word. As a career, I now work with Trans World Radio, an organization that not only reaches people in my country, Malawi, but spreads the gospel all over the world.

I still live a clean life before God, but now it is not just a matter of being a moral person. It is a matter of a relationship with Jesus Christ. With Him in my life, I don't need the crutches of support my friends turned to. I only need Him.

~ *Willie Kanthenga*

God's Reality Show

WITH THE POPULARITY of reality television shows, you can scarcely turn on the TV anymore without seeing someone eating bugs on a remote island or a person with a plastic bubble on his head containing thousands of bees. Is that reality?

Some time ago, someone told me that I don't know what reality is—that all Christians escape reality by clinging to some childish belief. "Christianity is just a crutch," they said, and in some ways they were right. I certainly needed a crutch, for I felt broken.

In fact, I had always felt broken. The one word that best described my life, from childhood on, was *loneliness*. My father left my family eight days after I was born, never to be heard from him again. It's lonely growing up without a dad.

My mother went from one relationship and place to another trying to fill the void in her life. By the time I graduated from high school, I had attended eighteen schools and lived in twenty-one different homes. I'd never been in one place long enough to find any relationships that lasted.

From watching my mother, I learned that people often turn to alcohol when relationships don't fill the void within them. Before the law kept children out of bars, my brother and I spent a lot of time in such establishments, just hanging out while our mother drank. Alcoholism added its own set of problems to our family: child abuse, sexual abuse, and the never-ending fights between our mother and her partner of the time.

Not too surprisingly, I wanted to escape. When I was little, I escaped into a fantasy world where I had a happy life, friends, a father who would come and rescue me, boyfriends, and a happy marriage. At the age of seventeen, though, I escaped into what I thought was the real world: I got married. I thought I'd immediately find love, security, and companionship. Marriage would fill the emptiness in my life, I was certain, and my loneliness would be forgotten. But it didn't work that way. After two failed marriages, I was still lonely and didn't know where to turn. If I hadn't had a son with my first husband, I would have ended my life. But somehow I couldn't see leaving my child with a legacy of suicide.

At one point, a friend had encouraged me to pray. For some reason, her words echoed through my mind: *"Pray, Jeanette!"*

My confused mind screamed, *"Pray to whom?"*

At that time, I wasn't sure God existed. Oh, I'd seen Billy Graham on TV. I'd attended a church occasionally in my messed-up childhood. I'd even been baptized. However, I thought, *"If there is a God, He is a long way off, and He certainly doesn't care about me."* Obviously, God either didn't care or had no power. Where was He when I was alone and scared? Where was He when I was sexually abused for nine years of my childhood? Where was He when my mom, her lovers, and her husbands would drink and fight?

I didn't have any answers, just an ache in my heart. But those two words wouldn't go away. *"Pray, Jeanette . . . Pray, Jeanette . . . Pray, Jeanette!"*

That night I experienced my first godly coincidence. I had put my son to bed, and the loneliness engulfed me. I felt as if the walls were closing in on me. I went to the small bookshelf that held the few books I owned. There on the shelf was my cousin's Bible. To this day, I don't know how it got there. I opened it to find a small pamphlet. The instructions on the first page grabbed my attention: "Where to find it if . . . you feel lonely," " . . . you feel God is far away," and " . . . you feel abandoned."

Whoa! "That's me!" I said. I opened the Bible and began to look up the references. The Bible verses seemed to be written just for me! As I read them, I began to sob uncontrollably.

For the first time in my life, I had to face the truth. I'd been raised in some difficult circumstances, yes, but I couldn't continue to blame others for my choices. I know I prayed many things in that moment, but one particular prayer stands out in my memory: "God, I have made a mess of my life. I am so tired of being lonely and trying to work this all out on my own. I give my life to You; if you can make something of it, it's Yours."

It's hard to explain how I felt afterward. I sat there on the floor for quite a while. The sobbing stopped. There was just silence, peaceful silence. I had no idea what the future would bring, but I felt the presence of God sitting with me. Suddenly my tiny apartment didn't seem to be so lonely anymore.

I didn't know it, but that night was the beginning of an amazing journey. This journey has taken me to the cross of Christ and to the very heart of the Father. The pages of the Bible now became alive with meaning. Every word of Jesus seemed clear, direct, and life changing.

One day I was reading Matthew 6:25–33. The heading in the Bible boldly stated "Do Not Worry." That was exactly what I had been doing. It was the first of the month, and I had received my paycheck. After paying the rent and my babysitter, the money in my hand amounted to only five dollars. *How can I stretch five dollars over two weeks? Do I buy gas or food?* The last two verses of Matthew 6 said, "Seek first His kingdom and His righteousness, and all these things will be given to you as well. Therefore do not worry about tomorrow."

I laid down my Bible and prayed, "Jesus, You say in Your Word that I am not to worry, so I give my worries to You, and I believe that You will meet our needs. Amen." Within days, the amount I needed to live on for the next two weeks came in, a little here and a little there. I was thrilled and amazed at how God had answered my prayer!

After becoming a Christian, I needed a social outlet. I wasn't interested in bars, but square dancing was good clean fun. I just needed a partner. Friends in my square-dancing group told me to call a young man who used to be a part of the group. I agonized over making that phone call because I felt awkward calling a man. When I finally called him, to my horror, I started crying shortly into the conversation. Somehow he understood me through the tears, and asked me to go out with him the next evening. I was startled and embarrassed. I said no, but he kept asking! Finally I agreed.

Malcolm had high morals and treated me with respect—a first for me. Several months later, I started to attend church with him. I was surprised that these people opened their arms to me. Since I'd always been a loner, I wasn't used to people welcoming me into their worlds. My son and I joined the church, and a year later, Mal and I were married there.

Mal was very active in the church and highly respected, but in our first year of marriage, I realized that something was missing in his life—he had no desire for the Word or for quiet time with God. When our family attended a Bible camp together, I asked him if he had ever asked Jesus into his life. He said he hadn't, and the very next morning he went forward and received Christ as his Savior.

During those years of my journey, I had no Christian women to mentor or disciple me. Instead, I sought answers at the public library, where I eagerly read books on faith. My desire to be a godly wife and mother and my lack of knowledge about how to be one led me to continue my quest for learning. And God was always with me—helping me and directing me to the right resources. I began reading the Bible and other Christian books, and I discovered a wealth of teaching available in Christian bookstores.

Those years of seeking by myself, led to my passion to mentor other women. I wanted other women who might be lonely to feel that they had someone besides God—someone on earth—on their team to help guide and encourage them. So I began working with women, leading Bible studies as well as helping them individually through their situations. I help them deal with the abuse they have suffered, aid them as they question "Where was God while this was going on?" and help them deal with their anger and grief. As my workload has grown, I have now become an unpaid member of my church's staff in the role of a pastoral counselor.

This journey has had its ups and downs, but the Father, whom Jesus introduced me to, has always been there. Sometimes I pinch myself and think, "*Am I just daydreaming again?*" The answer is *no*! My husband and our three children are a great gift from God. I often tell people, "If God can change my life, He can change yours. If He can take a lonely little girl and walk alongside her and give her purpose for living, He can do that for you, too."

And that reality — God's reality — is reality at its best!

~ *Jeanette M. Bakke*

New Life

"Is it time to have another child?" My husband Jim's question came out of nowhere one day when the youngest of our four children was three.

"No way!" I burst out. It was years before he brought up the subject again.

Our lives seemed almost ideal. My husband and I lived in the country with our four wonderful children, our dogs, cats, horses, chickens, and a garden. Nearby we had a loving, supportive church family. Four years earlier I had accepted Jesus as my Savior, and this personal relationship brought meaning and purpose to my life. The freedom of forgiveness brought a joy into my life I had never experienced.

Jim attended church with our family and spent time with Christian friends who often witnessed to him. He was riding the shirttails of my faith. Although he had not yet made this commitment to God, he was seeking, and many people were praying for him. I tried to encourage him by implementing God's plan for marriage: loving my husband and showing him that love, whether or not I agreed with him. That was not always easy for my strong-willed nature.

One morning I was chatting with a friend about the problems of having more children. Jim had brought up the subject again, and I'd explained, "It wouldn't be fair to the other children. They need us involved in their lives." I wouldn't even listen to his thoughts on it. That day on the phone I reiterated my opinion that families who experienced this situation often had unexpected complications. My children were ages eight to thirteen, and I had no intention of starting over with the baby scene. When I hung up, I was smug in my theory on family planning.

But seconds later, I was stopped in my tracks. It was as if I heard the Lord say, "If you are such a good wife, why won't you discuss the idea of more children with your husband, if that's what he wants?" The Lord cracked my hard heart and exposed my unwillingness to consider my husband's desire. Was this God's plan? Could the direction of my life change so radically in a few moments? The desire for another child could come only from God.

Soon we were expecting our fifth child. Our children shared our anticipation. For Jim and me, the pregnancy made us aware of the need for healing in our marriage and drew us closer together.

Six weeks before my delivery date, I tripped and fell. I rested a few days but seemed to be fine. But one Thursday morning, as I was preparing to leave for Bible study, I experienced signs of labor. My doctor was out of town until Saturday, and since nothing more developed, I decided to wait at home. On Saturday, when my doctor returned, he immediately ordered me into the hospital, where Benjamin Peter—little Benge—was born by cesarean section that night.

The doctor assured me that though Benge was cute as a button, a problem with his lungs meant he needed to stay in neonatal intensive care. She did not seem concerned, and the nurses were upbeat, so I didn't worry.

In fact, Benge had something called hyaline membrane disease. A chemical in his lungs had not developed enough to help him breathe. Jim left the hospital that night reluctant to tell me how serious the situation was. On the way home that night, he pulled over to the side of the road.

"God, if You will save our son, I will serve You the rest of my life," he bargained. Immediately he knew that God does not bargain. He prayed for forgiveness and gave his life to Christ. Assurance washed over him that God's will would be done for Benge.

When I was released from the hospital, Jim took me to visit our baby. He had needles and tubes everywhere, but I could hold him and feed him. He seemed very strong. I still did not perceive the danger. In fact, I didn't fully realize the grimness of the situation until we were getting ready to take him home and I read the list of procedures that had saved his life. My heart overflowed with gratitude for answered prayers—my husband's changed heart and our son's life.

The circumstances surrounding Benge's birth brought Jim and me together as one in Christ, and we have since been able to experience the marriage God intended for us. Jim grew in the Lord and has served Him as a teacher, counselor, church leader, and extension pastor.

Twenty-six years later, Jim and I walked into the hospital room where our son Ben held his son, Colin Scott. The scene filled us with precious memories of new life, both physical and spiritual.

∼ Marion E. Gorman

Safely in His Hands

"I'll go do it right now! What a hateful nag you are!" my father shouted. Even though I was only three years old, I knew my father was angry—though I had no idea why.

"Elsi, tell your father lunch will be at noon."

Now Mommy wasn't talking to Daddy. That meant she didn't love him. When I was bad, I'd noticed that Mommy and Daddy didn't talk to me because they didn't love me unless I was good. And when they had a fight, they didn't talk to each other. That's what happened when you were bad—nobody could love you.

It was very lonely, being bad.

"Daddy," I whispered, "Mommy says—"

"I know," her Daddy snapped. "Tell your mother I'll be outside, putting up the screens."

The door slammed behind him. Mommy started grabbing plates off the table. I slipped into my room to find a book big enough to hide in and clutched it tightly. Gazing at the pictures and remembering the story, I drifted into a safer world.

Then I heard a shout from outside. "Molly Jean! I've fallen!"

Molly Jean was Mommy. We ran for the backyard.

Daddy had been taking down storm windows when the ladder broke. His face looked funny, and he was moaning.

"Poor Daddy," I said, patting his face. But Daddy didn't smile at me like normal. The ambulance came and I watched as men put Daddy on a bed in the car.

"Can I do anything?" a neighbor asked.

"Watch Elsi for me," Mommy said, and she climbed into the car with Daddy.

For the next few months, I was passed around among neighbors and friends. I saw my mother every day, but she always seemed to be thinking of something else. No one bothered to explain the problem to me. I knew I must have been bad if Daddy was so mad at me that he didn't even come home! And Mommy didn't stay home, either. I figured I was the worst little girl in the world since neither of my parents wanted to be with me.

Years later, I still mourn what happened to the child I was. During the months of my father's hospitalization, I felt deserted. In the course of being passed about so much, I was also molested, and I developed the ability to dissociate.

My parents used to tell me, "You're an unnatural child!" Or "We should take you back to the hospital and trade you in!"

Oh, they were joking, of course. At least, that's what they'd say if you asked. But those comments—along with ones like "You'd be so pretty if you wore contacts" and "Only a 99 percent on the test? What did you miss?"—made it clear I just wasn't up to their standards. So when I met some Christians in college who told me that God was my loving Father, I wasn't impressed. All I needed was another authority figure to tell me all the ways I was doing things wrong.

"You're His child, and He loves you!" they insisted.

Me? A child of God? No way! I thought. And if I am His child, then I'm an unnatural child, the one who isn't wanted.

But these friends accepted me, and slowly I began to respond to that. And you know something? God's promises—the ones about His love, anyway—don't have any "ifs" in them. Sure, *if* we obey, we will be blessed. *If* we are humble, He will use us. But His love? There's not an *if* to be found. He just loves us.

When I began to realize that, I turned to Christ for love. And He accepted me, unconditionally. My soul was saved, but my heart remained untrusting, well defended. I accepted His love but maintained a "We'll see" attitude. And that lack of trusting love eventually led to two divorces, which only reinforced the lesson I'd learned in my childhood: I was unlovable.

Some years later, I went to a worship service. "Sometimes we wonder, *where is God?*" the leader said to us. "Where was God when this tragedy happened? How could He allow it to happen?"

He paused for a moment while we thought. Then he continued, "If you can't see how God could have allowed something, I would like you to close your eyes and visualize Jesus in that situation. What is He doing?"

Immediately I thought about the child I had been. How would it have helped that little girl to have Jesus standing by, watching all the bad things that happened to her? Wouldn't that just make it worse? I called up the scene in my mind: the blue sky, the broken ladder, the little girl running toward circumstances she could not comprehend. An unexpected emotion crashed through me—I felt sorry for my mother.

I had never thought of it from her point of view. She was young, without a support system, and her husband had just been seriously hurt. Worse, their argument had probably made her feel responsible for his injury. Her husband faced losing a leg, or worse. And she had a whiny three-year-old making demands. I had no way of explaining to my mother what I was feeling and what was happening to me, and she never thought to explain why my father didn't come home for so long. She put me in the care of people she trusted as she also tried to deal with the aftermath of the accident. The poor woman!

I clenched my fists to hold back the tears as I was over-whelmed with compassion for both mother and child, caught in such a hard place. As the Holy Spirit worked in my heart, I became free to love. The change in me was amazing, but I still couldn't totally let go of my fears.

For instance, one day when I was at a teachers' reception in the school where I worked, a colleague asked, "Why are you holding on to that woman's bag?"

I looked at my hand, which was clenched securely around the strap of my friend's purse, and took a deep breath. "I have panic attacks in groups," I explained. "Even in faculty meetings. But we're required to be here. So my friend is helping me stay grounded enough to function." I shifted my grip on the bag, noting that I needed to trim my nails, as they were cutting my palms.

When I wasn't clutching bags, I was clutching other things or clenching my fists. As I sought help, I learned in therapy that I was really holding onto myself. If I held on tightly enough, my tears and my fears would not escape and crush me.

"I hate being like this!" I told my therapist. "I feel so stupid, so incompetent and . . . and *unlovable*!"

"Let's try something," she suggested. "Can you think back to the first time you felt that way? Let's try to put Jesus in that scene. Try to create a picture in your mind."

But I wasn't listening to her any more. I suddenly felt Jesus was there, reaching out His hand. I didn't see His face, and I don't think I actually heard His voice. But I knew what He was saying: "Do you love Me?"

I nodded.

"Do you trust Me?"

I nodded again.

"If you trust Me, take My hand."

I froze, fists clenched.

He didn't coax me. He just waited, hand outstretched.

In order to take His hand, I would have to release what I was holding. Could I risk what might happen? I vaguely heard my therapist talking in the background. But I wasn't paying attention. I was trying to decide what to do. Dare I take His hand? Dare I not? He was waiting. I have no idea how long it took me to uncurl my body, open my hand, and reach out. As my fingers closed around air, tears started to flow. I felt free.

Later, at school, the art teacher said, "What happened to you? You seem more relaxed, happier. And you don't keep your fists tight anymore."

In taking His hand, I turned my back on fear and withdrawal. I allowed Him to lead me into the safety of His life and light. And I truly believed I was His child. I became whole in His love.

The Elsi from my childhood doesn't haunt me anymore. I am loved. I am accepted by the Creator of the universe. I have been changed by the Savior of the world. I have a heavenly Father, one I call Abba, Daddy.

~ *Elsi Dodge*

An Instrument God Uses

DON'T TELL ME that God doesn't possess an exquisite sense of humor! Every single thing I ever wanted from the world, He eventually gave me in overflowing measure in the Christian sphere.

All I remember from my early years was a parental battleground. I was born into an ethnic family, one that grew out of an arranged marriage. My father emigrated from Damascus, Syria, to a tiny, backwash town in northern Queensland, Australia. He was a successful businessman, and at age sixty, he married a much younger Greek woman, Angeliki, who was from Alexandria. That made me a Syro-Phoenician, or a Greco-Syrian, by blood. Looking back, I recollect my mother's abject loneliness, as one day I heard her crying and cursing Captain Cook for discovering Australia.

At age six, I became fascinated by a world-renowned violinist I saw in a movie. I begged my mother to buy me a tin violin I had seen in our local barbershop, and then I cried because it didn't have a bow. She later purchased the genuine article for me, and I began violin lessons. Though I loved my violin, I remember sometimes looking out the window, wistfully watching other boys kicking a ball around while I stayed indoors, practicing scales.

When I was ten years old, my parents died within six months of each other and I became an orphan. I was devastated. My nights were full of dreams of my mother turning away from me, not knowing who I was. But soon movies and radio filled that aching emptiness and forged my dreams. I determined I would earn fame and grasp security by becoming an actor and traveling the world.

At boarding school, the violin saved me from being bullied because by then I had learned to jazz up all the latest pop songs. Fortunately, that entertained the older, meaner, tougher boys, and gave me safety and status in their eyes.

I read children's books about great Bible heroes, and I thought it'd be wonderful to hear God speak. My mother had awakened an interest in God in me. Being of the Orthodox persuasion, she used to pray before an icon. After she died, I continued to recite prayers in Greek, as she had, until I realized that if God was as smart as I thought He was, then He would understand English just as well.

So I found comfort in reading about Bible heroes. I gave assent to the Ten Commandments—after all, following the commandments was similar to "playing by the rules." And I had to do that in my music. My music led me to pray, too. I also would often pray before an icon, regularly asking favors to help me in violin exams and competitions. When I was in my teens, I finally played a solo in the Mendelssohn Violin Concerto, with full orchestral accompaniment. I was deeply affected by this success and agreed with my teacher that musically, I'd gone as far as I could go where I was. The next step was to say farewell to my small town forever and take further studies with a top violin master at the Sydney Conservatorium of Music.

In the big city, I worked at any odd jobs that gave me enough money to pay for lessons, as well as plenty of time for violin practice. To gain stage experience, I joined a concert party that traveled to outback areas to raise money for sick children. However, we soon discovered the country folk weren't too impressed by classical music. A Western show had toured the same areas just before our group arrived. Though the Western show had played in venues filled to capacity with standing room only, we were lucky to gain a three-quarter capacity. Still, the audiences enjoyed my renditions of Debussy's *Flight of the Bumblebee* and Manuel de Falla's fiery *Danse Espagnole*. At the time, I never guessed I'd later return to many of those towns for an entirely different purpose.

Back in Sydney, my career was going according to plan. I was just beginning to make a name in classical music circles when things radically changed. At the guesthouse where I boarded, a distinguished old gentleman named Arthur Coster took an interest in me. His brother was a well-known London photographer who wanted to get some shots of me with the violin. From then on, Mr. Coster often asked me to have coffee with him. During that time, he often brought up the subject of spiritual things. I respected his wisdom and felt fond of him since I really didn't have any friends in this big, busy city.

Mr. Coster often talked about salvation. I wondered how he knew about such things, and he'd always say, "The Bible says so." That may well be, I conceded, but I felt I was already okay with God. Hadn't He helped me through the tight spots in my career? Hadn't I played gratis for numerous charitable functions? And when I was a baby, I'd been wholly immersed in the waters of baptism by a Greek Orthodox priest. As a twelve-year-old, I'd served as an altar boy and had been sprinkled by an Episcopalian priest—probably as a backup measure! Therefore, I felt reasonably sure that God would take all these fine things into account.

To please the old man, I finally agreed to attend an evangelistic crusade with him. The services were held in the Sydney Town Hall, and I had to join the overflow crowds that filled the chapter house of St. Andrew's Cathedral, where the message was relayed over loudspeakers. It was strange, I thought, sitting there listening to a voice telling me I was a sinner and that Jesus Christ had willingly given His life, dying on my behalf. Did all these people around me feel as uncomfortable as I did?

Somehow, during all those years I'd spent as an altar boy helping with Holy Communion, I'd never heard the Gospel story like this. Now it seemed to incriminate me. I'd always assumed I had to improve myself—to do the best with what I had in life. But for the first time, the truth sank in, and I realized that Jesus had done it all. He had deliberately given up His perfect life to save me and forgive me my sins. In my mind's eye, I saw Him hanging on that awful cross. It broke my heart . . . and my pride.

When the voice from the loudspeakers asked those who wanted to receive Christ as their Savior to stand, a power raised me to my feet. I knew it might be the last time I would ever get such an opportunity, so I gave my whole being to the Lord. Nobody counseled me, but I knew things were different. It was a fresh start.

Soon after, I was the guest violinist at a church function. The program also featured a guest speaker, and everything she said touched a chord in my heart. I approached her afterward and told her about my experience of becoming a true believer. She told me how much she had enjoyed my violin music, and she asked for my phone number. The next day, her son, who worked with an organization called Youth for Christ (YFC), called me and arranged an audition for me to play my violin for their ministry. From that time on, I was swept up in service for the Lord. I played my violin, sang in a quartet, and helped the presenter on the Sydney YFC's weekly radio program.

In that YFC auditorium I met my wife. We entered Bible college together to prepare for whatever service the Lord had planned for us. We were invited by an American evangelist to be on his music team, and we traveled with him for five years. Then finally, because I couldn't stop sharing the Good News, we became itinerant evangelists ourselves. My wife, who is an artist, sketches as I preach. At times, I even still pull out the violin that led me to Mr. Coster, whose actions led me to Christ. We are amazed at the opportunities the Lord has given us to share the Gospel. We are privileged to appear on a weekly radio program and as occasional guests on Christian television. We have toured and preached the simple gospel message in Australia and around the world, and we regularly minister in Southeast Asia in Buddhist schools, hospitals, prisons, and shopping malls.

As I look back, I recall something my mother shared with me before she died. She said she'd had a vision of Jesus standing by her bed. He'd told her that one day God would use me. As a child, I had no idea what this could mean, and I'm not sure my mother did either. I'm sure she had no idea what path she was setting me on when she bought me that little tin violin, and then the real instrument with the bow.

Now it strikes me deeply when those words come back to me as I stand before an audience of people from different cultures and all walks of life, telling them how they can experience real peace in their lives by finding salvation through faith in the Lord Jesus Christ.

Jesus' yoke is easy, and His burden is light. I no longer feel I must play by a set of rules that this world tries to impose on me. Yes, the God who sees widows and orphans saw fit to take one little fellow who had big dreams and a longing in his heart, and He fulfilled over and above every worldly aspiration in a deeper, more spiritual, and satisfying way that will count for eternity. God can use any instrument to reach us, and in my case, His instrument was a violin.

~ *George Elias Galieh*

Pilgrimage Home

SURROUNDED BY A sea of unfamiliar faces, I searched for the friend who had invited me to this Thanksgiving dinner. Though I couldn't find her, another young woman I knew approached me with a big smile. Obviously excited by my presence at church, she greeted me and then gushed, "So when did you get saved?"

"Saved?" I asked.

By the flustered look on her face, I knew she was embarrassed by her assumption. "We'll talk about it later," she said and scurried away.

After a while, I found the person I was looking for and followed her to the basement of the country church, a room she called the "fellowship hall." I hadn't been in a place like this since I was a little girl holding a white lily and preparing for Holy Thursday services. In those days, I'd loved sitting in the pews, gazing at the stained-glass windows, and talking to Jesus. Little by little, though, that faith had eroded. During high school, I had started running away from God.

We sat down at one of the long narrow tables, and while everyone else chatted, I mulled over the other woman's words. *What does it mean to be saved?* I wondered. *What do I need to be saved from?*

Sure, I had led a somewhat wild life by some people's standards, but it wasn't as bad as others I knew. At nineteen I'd quit school to travel through Europe with my boyfriend, though he and I had parted company in Switzerland. While he headed east to India, I went south to France. From there I hitchhiked the autobahn of Germany and basked in the sunshine of the Balearic Islands in Spain and the Canaries off the west coast of Africa. I traveled through all of Europe, seeking fun and adventure. I encountered a few storms but most of it was exciting. It was an escapade of parties, new friends, and romance. After visiting some of the best-known museums in the world, I changed my college major to study art. Back in the States, I transferred to one of the most liberal colleges on the East Coast.

But saved . . . from what?

I recalled a conversation with another student. He had said, "You're worshiping the creation rather than the creator." His words struck a chord at the time, but I ignored them. Now I wondered if they had something to do with being saved.

As I looked around the room, feeling uncomfortable, I thought I wouldn't mind being saved or delivered from this odd assortment of Christians. I liked the college meetings I'd just started attending that had a religious focus, but these people seemed so different. I couldn't wait to start eating.

When the pastor stood up, I figured he would pray and then we would begin to feast. When he finished praying, I opened my eyes and was ready to dive in, but then the woman next to me started praying. Her voice filled the room with a ring of authority, so I sat up and listened.

"Know that the Lord, He is God: it is he that hath made us, and not we ourselves; we are his people, and the sheep of his pasture. Enter into His gates with thanksgiving, and into His courts with praise: be thankful unto him, and bless his name. For the Lord is good; his mercy is everlasting; and his truth endureth to all generations" (Psalm 100:3–5).

It was like a thunderbolt had struck. I felt as if God had spoken directly into my heart. Though He had created me, I was still trying to run the show. As the food was passed around, I was hardly paying attention—I was contemplating an inner, spiritual hunger that I'd been suppressing.

As a relatively good Catholic schoolgirl, I'd grown up with a consciousness of sin. When I first started attending college, I questioned everything that I knew to be right and did things that inwardly I knew to be wrong. I'd suppressed the truth in my own heart, blinded by peer pressure and the desire to do things my way. Yet there had been a lot more stormy seas than I cared to admit, and lately the reality of my lifestyle had come crashing down around me.

Perhaps that's why I'd accepted an old boyfriend's invitation to attend a student Christian group on campus—I'd promised to go if he would leave me alone, but had started to enjoy the meetings. Then I'd gotten invited to this Thanksgiving dinner. Just as the Pilgrims had set out so long ago, not sure where they would end up, but still seeking to serve God, perhaps I'd started on my own journey to find God in some new spiritual land.

It's not like I'd never searched for God before. Through my years of wandering, I had tried to fill a void in my soul by not only wandering through the pleasures of this world, but also exploring other religious philosophies—that of the Buddha, of Krishna, of Eastern mysticism, Tarot cards, astrology, numerology, and so on. They left me hollow. I'd run around the world, but I couldn't escape myself. In the past year, I'd started spiraling downward into depression. I'd broken off another live-in relationship and it had devastated me. Other men didn't fill the void, either. I spent a lot of time alone working on my art. Some of it was good, but I had to admit other pieces were strange and spooky. For an assignment I painted a self-portrait that looked like an African talisman. Later, I realized it represented my internal struggle between good and evil.

And that's the very conflict I was engaged in now. While someone passed the potatoes, a decision was being required of me. *Was I going to follow God's way or my own?*

I could take the leap of faith and trust God with my life, or I could continue to make my own choices and do whatever I wanted. Since doing my own thing had already led to a big dead end, I decided to try His way. I felt compelled to surrender my will, and so I said yes to God.

I realized that not only was I a sinner, but without God I was never going to be whole or complete. I needed Him in my life to fill up the emptiness and longing.

As I passed the celery and thought about my life, I understood that God had never really let go of me. The whole time I was running away, He was gently calling me. I had seen evidence of Him at every turn. In Europe as I traveled with a group of hippies, He saved us from being thrown into jail on several occasions—such as when I crossed from Morocco to Spain carrying contraband. When I returned home, I heard horror stories of Americans who had been put in prison for years without a trial. I thanked God then for rescuing me, even though I wasn't following His ways.

Other occurrences flashed across my mind: the time He saved me from being raped, the time He kept me from being killed when I dove off a high cliff into a river below, and the numerous times I denied Him. God was willing to forgive me for everything, if I was willing to accept Him into my life and believe in Him. He had been gently trying to bring me back into the fold, but I until now I hadn't been willing.

It all started to come together. In some ways, I felt like Dorothy in *The Wizard of Oz*. I had traveled far from home, only to discover what I'd been looking for was in my own back yard. As I began eating turkey and stuffing, I felt different—lighter and happier. After dinner, I turned to the woman sitting next to me, the one who had spoken the unusual prayer, and I thanked her for it.

The evening of that Thanksgiving dinner, I felt as if I had journeyed across the Atlantic on my own rocky pilgrimage and finally, after many storms, landed safely on shore. I now understood what it meant to be "saved," and I knew what I was saved from—my foolishness, self-will, and sin. Like the Pilgrims, I had been searching for religious freedom, but my journey brought me right back home to Jesus. I had the best reason in the world to be thankful, not only for what God provided physically, but also for the provision of His Son.

~ *Anita Estes*

Losing Control to Find It

I WAS HAVING a nervous breakdown. With my two-month-old baby in my arms, I had made the mistake of watching the local news. For the third time that summer, a child had been accidentally left in a day-care van and had died from heat exhaustion.

"Why are you crying?" my husband asked, putting his arm around me. Between the hiccups and sobs, I couldn't speak. I looked at the baby in my arms and then pointed to the television. He understood and turned it off.

"No more news until the postpartum depression goes away," he said and leaned over to kiss my cheek.

But it wasn't postpartum depression that made me cry. It was my constant fear that someone I loved would be taken away and I'd be helpless to stop it. He didn't know how often I felt sick from worry when he was late coming home from work. Within minutes, I'd imagine him dead and buried and myself a tragic widow. Then, in the middle of my drama, he'd walk in with the dry cleaning or the milk we needed. Now, thanks in part to the local news, my imagined tragedies included my helpless baby girl.

Knowing I'd be going back to work soon and leaving her at a day care made the news report even more terrifying. It didn't take much to picture the tiny white casket I was sure she'd end up in. It would be all my fault for not controlling the situation so I could protect her, not anticipating the accident that caused her death, and not having the right contingency plan in place.

I developed these obsessive and controlling tendencies early in life as I grew up in an alcoholic family that was always on the verge of poverty. It didn't take long to decide this was not how I was going to live the rest of my life or raise my own children. I figured if I had control over everything and everyone, I could make sure those childhood issues didn't crop up in my adult life. Then those I cared about would never be hurt. I juggled all of this, and life was not much fun for me or my loved ones.

Then one day my fears hit close to home. A train slipped off its tracks, and several cars flipped and caught fire. A couple of women from our community had been on that train, along with their daughters. Flames completely engulfed the part of the train where the children had been riding, and their mothers could only watch helplessly. A friend who knew one of the families told me of how the mothers had knelt beside the burning train and prayed.

"It's just crazy that they did nothing but pray while their children were dying right in front of them!" I told my husband.

"It's not like they could have . . ."

"I would have," I cut him off. "I would have done something."

The more I thought about those moms, the angrier I became. They should have saved their daughters. I quickly made it their fault so I could assure myself that it would never happen to me. I would protect my daughter at all costs. Right then I announced that she'd never sleep away from me and she'd certainly never set foot on a train.

Over the next days, stories began circulating about the children who had died. One man told of how the youngest of the girls used to talk to him about Jesus. He was so struck by her childlike faith that he was moved to "accept Christ" that very day. I rolled my eyes and wondered what was wrong with these people. Couldn't they see that that was just a nice story to help everyone deal with the pain? As more and more people told stories about these little girls, one thing that always came up was their love for Jesus and their love for talking about Him to everyone.

Whatever gets them through the day is fine with me, I thought. Then I heard something I could not believe. The parents of the girls wanted to have the funerals televised.

"That is morbid! Are they trying to make a spectacle? What are they thinking?" My husband agreed it was strange and we decided not to watch.

The next day I asked my friend, "Why would they share such a personal thing, especially on TV?"

She said, "They're trying to bring something good out of this. They hope to help others by explaining how God is helping them through it and giving them peace."

They had to be kidding. I couldn't imagine what good could come of this tragedy and how anyone could feel a hint of peace when their children had just died. Nonetheless, I was curious. I taped the funeral, and that evening, I watched it alone.

After a few songs, the father of the deceased children stood and spoke. He was remarkably composed except for the occasional silent tear. I don't recall exactly what he said, but his voice was strong and unwavering and the ideas his words conveyed had a profound effect on me.

He said something like, "They aren't really our children, they're God's. We're grateful we got to have them as long as we did even though it hurts that we can't keep them longer. But, we know it's not our decision and it's completely out of our control. We know our daughters are with Jesus now and are happy. So, we're sad for ourselves, not for them."

Then he said the thing that really got me. "We trust and believe that God protected their hearts and minds from what happened on that train. We know they didn't have fear or pain because God was always with them, even when we couldn't be. Knowing this gives us peace."

This man had exactly what I was missing. I needed to know my daughter was protected even when I wasn't with her. I knew my brave words were fake and I couldn't always save her from everything. If something ever should happen, I wanted to have the same confidence and peace that this man had.

Without meaning to, I said out loud, "You'll have to do it because I can't." It was unexpected and strange, but it felt like a weight lifted from my shoulders. I paid little attention. I turned off the TV and began to fix dinner.

I tried to ignore what had happened, but eventually I began to suspect that I'd spoken to God. I couldn't shake that feeling of weight being lifted from me and wondered if I'd imagined it. The stress was getting to me and I feared I was going crazy. Ridiculous standards for housekeeping, worry about the finances, obsession over maintaining the schedule, and manipulating what others thought of me was exhausting. The new baby and recent return to work had taken me over the edge. I felt foolish and didn't tell anyone, but slowly and cautiously, I talked to God a little more.

I simply thought, "I'm tired and I can't keep this up. I'm really scared and worried. I think I need Your help." As I talked, that feeling of freedom came again. I still wasn't sure if I was imagining it, but this time I didn't care. As the overwhelming burden of responsibility for everyone and everything became a little lighter, I realized maybe I didn't have to do it all myself. Was it possible that God would take care of me and my loved ones? I was curious about this new way of thinking.

With no idea what to expect, I went to church. I was testing those new feelings and thoughts and wanted to see what would happen. That morning, it felt like the preacher was talking to me. He made sense and what he said related to my situation. I figured this was mere coincidence but went back to hear more. It wasn't a coincidence, though, and I began going to church every week expecting to hear things that were meaningful and would make a difference to me. I learned what it meant to have God in my life, and I finally learned what that man meant when he said the little girl's words moved him to "accept Christ." He simply decided that life with God is better than life without God. I agreed.

That was nine years ago. Today, I'm still a control freak. I'm convinced it's not all bad. I'm very organized and productive. My home runs smoothly and is not chaotic. I'm a good planner and a great multitasker. But there is one major difference between the old me and the new one.

Now when life gets overwhelming, or when bad things happen, I know whose job it is to sort it all out. Rather than taking it on myself to plan for every unknown crisis or fix things that are beyond my control, I remember that He is God, I'm not, and He can handle all that stuff.

It's not easy to admit that I don't have complete control, but it's much harder trying to live life pretending I do. Something happened that day I told God I needed help: He took over. I've finally found the same confidence and peace those mothers demonstrated the day they knelt beside that burning train . . . and prayed.

~ *Lynn M. Stout*

When God Enters the Stepfamily

"I'M EXHAUSTED. THERE'S no hope."

Finally, I'd said the words out loud, relieved to let go of the daily fight to fix our emotionally spent family. This was not what I wanted, but now I sat slumped in the corner of the beige sofa with my hands over my eyes, resigned to what I believed was the truth. After seven very difficult years, I saw no reason to believe our stepfamily would survive. We simply didn't know how to make family a happy place. The only thing left to do was to admit we had failed at being a family—again.

The clock struck midnight, but I'd given up on the Cinderella happily-ever-after ending. The glass slipper belonged on someone else's foot. My Prince Charming was behaving more like a male prototype of the unkind stepmother, unwilling to give genuine love to his two stepchildren. What really ticked me off was that I hadn't seen this coming before I married this man. My children wanted his approval. Life just didn't make sense anymore.

On the outside we looked like any other family. We went to work, involved ourselves in the community, kept up with the children's activities, lived in a nice home, and had a respectable list of friends and neighbors. We were all wearing masks.

Behind the doors of our house was a performance-based love, way too many heated arguments, and too much alcohol to deaden my husband's emotional pain—the pain loaded with guilt and regret for no longer living with his three children.

For the longest time I didn't realize how big a problem this really was. Living with his stepchildren, my children, was a daily reminder to Charlie of what he had lost. He kept those feelings under wraps, and they only showed up in unkind ways. We only knew that most days, his after-work conversation centered on the children who did not live with us, not on the ones who did. *What are they doing? Why don't they call? Do they still love me?*

He thought that adopting my daughter and son would improve his relationship with them, but things still didn't move ahead as we'd expected. It wasn't long before I heard those five words, "Blood runs thicker than water," all over again. That's all it took to kick another argument into high gear and make me question whether I should stay in this marriage or get out.

"I married you; not your children," he blurted out one day.

I was stunned. "When you married me you knew I had children. By saying yes to me you said yes to them, or at least I presumed you did. That's simply not fair!"

I was mad at myself. I was doubly mad at my husband. But by now life was even more complicated. We had a daughter together. She didn't deserve to have her family torn apart any more than my older children needed one more broken family. None of us wanted a miserable life.

No matter how bad things got, another divorce didn't seem like the right answer to our problems, but I knew something had to change.

The day after I'd given up hope, I was visiting with a few moms while our five-year-old daughter attended her ballet lesson. We spent the time sharing stories about everything from ear infections to family drama to Sunday picnics while the girls flitted about the dance floor. Then the conversation shifted rather abruptly.

"I don't know where I would be today if I didn't know God cares about my family," one mom said to me. "Do you like to study?

"Yes," I replied, "I like to learn new things."

"Would you consider coming to Bible study with me? Every week I take home something that applies to my family that I've learned from studying the Bible. I belong to a group called Bible Study Fellowship. It meets once a week on Thursday. There's a social part, too. Once a month we have a luncheon."

"I don't know very much about the Bible," I said. "That's an interesting idea. Could I call you in a couple days and let you know?"

I'd tried to read the Bible. I'd gotten about as far as Deuteronomy, become frustrated, and given up on the big book. I didn't come from a family where church was a priority. My mother believed flying saucers and spiritual mediums were real, and my father sometimes played the role of a fortuneteller for people who visited him. When I was a child, the whole Christian thing seemed odd and a bit frightening. My parents did let me attend the Good News Club when I was in grade school. I remember liking the Bible stories, but I was still just a kid with no follow-up at home.

Now, all these years later, after one failed marriage and my second one a mess, a friend was asking me to learn about God.

Was my new friend right? Was there something for me in God's word? My idea of God was that of a vague far-away deity full of Ten Commandments—not a God who could possibly love me.

Maybe it was time I found out the truth for myself. I had to admit I'd been stirred by the ads on the radio the past couple weeks. They told of Easter programs taking place at local churches. I was thirty-three years old, the same age Jesus was when He hung on the cross, and I didn't know who He really was.

Was I good enough for heaven or not? In the back of my mind I thought perfect people went to heaven, and I sure wasn't perfect! I doubted whether divorced people would be accepted through the pearly gates. A little self-talk kicked in. *Get brave, Maxine. It's time you figured this part of life out. For sure, you're going to die some day. Everybody does. You've got nothing to lose and maybe, just maybe, you'll hear something to get happy about.*

I called my friend the next day. "I'll go to Bible study with you on Thursday.

"Great!" she said. "Meet me in the church foyer."

The sun shone brightly on that morning. Jesus, God's own Son, was shining even brighter. I discovered that Paul called himself a "chief sinner." He didn't live a perfect life but he was forgiven. To my surprise I was told everybody in Heaven was once a sinner! I learned that God loved divorced people as much as He loved Abraham, Mary, and Joseph. God wanted me in Heaven in spite of my imperfect past. My sins were forgivable, too.

What a relief to hear about being loved with an everlasting love. I'd never heard about everlasting love before. The love I had for my children was the closest reference I had to that kind of love. Love from other people had always felt conditional to me. I happily accepted Jesus as my personal Savior that day.

I went home with a changed heart, a new attitude, and a renewed hope. With God on my side I no longer felt alone. I believed God would give me answers to the problems that were suffocating our family. I deliberately applied what I was learning first to myself and then, even though it wasn't always easy, passed the unconditional love and forgiveness I'd received onto my husband and my children.

A lot of life is personal choice. Once I felt forgiven, I was ready to choose, on purpose, to forgive my husband for the words he'd said that hurt me so much. Getting even with him was no longer part of my agenda. I saw him as someone in need of God's love, too. To my surprise, the day I said, "I forgive you for not fully loving my children," God began to move in his heart. His words began to improve! He began to feel better about himself and about us as a family.

I looked forward to Thursday mornings with Bible Study Fellowship, eager to learn more and more about God's character and how biblical people lived. Six months later, our family started attending a Christ-centered church, and my husband accepted Jesus into his heart. Half a dozen couples began to pray for us and include us in their lives.

We were asked to Bible study groups and social events in their homes and at the church. The new friends were good role models for us. Best of all, we were learning about the Lord and His love for our family. Our children started to see God at work in our home. In turn, they got excited about the youth activities at the church. My decision to accept Jesus changed the direction of our whole family.

Old habits die hard. We still experienced times when patterns of the past popped up, but they were getting fewer and farther between. The hope we'd found was real hope. God is who the Bible declares Him to be. All of us had a part to play, and we all grabbed on to the idea that working together and applying God's plan at home would give us our best shot at a good family.

Today, our children are all grown. Those raised in our home are walking by faith in their own families. God has allowed me to encourage other families, like ours, who have been wounded by divorce and remarriage. It's nice to know God doesn't waste a hurt. Instead, He turns those wounded spaces into opportunities to bring hope to others.

God's work in my husband's life didn't stop either. Today, he is an ordained minister, on staff with Crown Financial Ministries, and spreads hope to many broken people.

Living in a stepfamily isn't easy. It's the hardest thing I've ever done. Sometimes I wanted to quit. I'm glad I didn't. I'm also glad God used those places I couldn't fix with my own strength to bring me to the end of my efforts and into relationship with Him. Through all the rough times, I can look back and see God's hand on our family. I know if He can move in our lives, He will also bring hope and healing to other people who find themselves feeling as desperate as I did before I knew Jesus was my friend and Savior.

$\sim$ *Maxine Marsolini*

A Different Destiny

"OKAY, LET ME see your hands." I ordered the next teen in line to turn up her palms for my inspection. Peering closely, I delivered my verdict. "You've got an interesting lifeline; looks like you're going to have a couple kids, too. What day did you say you were born?"

"Read mine next!" Classmates crowded in, begging me to chart their horoscopes. I had no time for that, though. I was already booked. Some teachers down the hall wanted me to predict their futures, too, and I didn't want to miss my whole lunch. Pushing past my friends, I tapped on the faculty-lounge door and stepped inside.

At the moment, I was the most popular person in school. Just fifteen, I already had an uncanny knack for supernatural insight, and my reputation was growing.

For as long as I could remember, I had been drawn to the occult. Eerie books and movies thrilled me with their unexplained, spooky tales. Tarot cards, ESP, Ouija boards, horoscopes—anything strange fueled my hunger to learn more.

As I contemplated my own future, astrology seemed to clear the murky phases of life ahead: meeting my perfect mate, choosing a career path to maneuver, planning a family yet unborn.

I believed astrology was my guide. Born in mid-May, I fell under the sign of Taurus, the Bull, which along with my being redheaded guaranteed a strong will and stubborn streak, I figured. My horoscope directed me in using my natural personality strengths to control my own destiny and influence those around me. When I started following my horoscope religiously, I found it remarkably accurate. Armed with this revelation, I quickly became the poster girl for astrology and fortune telling.

Welcoming my newfound popularity, I impressed my peers by charting their horoscopes and reading their palms. I was a good kid—no drugs, no drinking, no sleeping around. I viewed my astrological ability as a gift and tried to help people. I believed there was a god and that I was going to heaven when I died.

I was an enlightened individual.

A simple invitation changed my life forever. A girlfriend asked if I would like to spend Saturday night at her house, and in the morning, she invited me to church.

"Sure," I agreed. Why not? I attended services every Easter and Christmas and had seldom missed vacation Bible school when I was a kid.

I had never visited this church, but the town was small enough that as I walked in, I immediately recognized several people in the congregation. Settling into a pew, I turned my attention to the pulpit.

The message that morning was on astrology and the occult. The pastor began to talk, and the longer he spoke, the more I squirmed. Some of the teens were glancing my way and whispering. "That's the girl who reads palms at school!"

First, I was humiliated. Then I was furious.

The pastor preached on.

When the service ended, my Taurus-stubborn pride refused to let me leave without speaking my mind. Stepping through some side doors, I saw the pastor striding down the hall in front of me. I reached out and grabbed his sleeve. He whirled around.

"Preacher, is anything really wrong with astrology?" I demanded.

He surprised me by grinning and saying, "Come with me."

Leading the way to his office, the pastor had me sit down beside him at his desk. Then he began to show me all the verses he could find in God's Word that spoke against my recent activities. He read a lot of verses including Isaiah 47:13–14, which promised dire consequences for astrologers and stargazers, and pointed out that such people can't even save themselves.

I flinched. Some of the scriptures said that God's anger burned against people like me. Never had I considered that God might be angry with me. I was trying to help people!

Verse after verse condemned me: "Anyone who does these things is detestable to the LORD" (Deuteronomy 18:12).

It was like a curtain raised. I sat ashen-faced, struck with an enormous truth. I was in major trouble. And I knew it to the very core of my being.

As the pastor prayed, I asked Jesus to forgive my sins—especially my dabbling in the occult. Relief flooded through my body as I felt God's smile and an indescribable peace settled on me.

It doesn't take a fortuneteller to see what came next. Out went the horoscopes; in came the Bible. The Bright Morning Star, not a counterfeit, now charted my future.

A couple of months later, the kids in our youth group were talking about how we each got saved. My pastor looked at me and said, "Hey, you know why I grinned so big when you yanked on my sleeve that Sunday?" Turns out, he had a different sermon prepared, but he had woken up Saturday night with an unshakable impression that someone in the congregation the next morning would need to hear the truth about astrology.

"For God so loved . . ." a teenager, that He changed a sermon and saved the course of her life, and beyond.

~ *Cheryl Gochnauer*

Contributors

Candy Arrington ("A Whisper in the Silence") is the coauthor of *Aftershock: Help, Hope, and Healing in the Wake of Suicide*, and is a contributor to numerous anthologies. Her other publishing credits include *Today's Christian, Focus on the Family,* and *Writer's Digest.*

Jeanette M. Bakke ("God's Reality Show") is married and is the mother of three grown children and the grandmother of two boys. Her passion is to mentor women in the faith by teaching one-on-one classes in speaking and writing.

Alma Barkman ("Looking for My Father") is a freelance writer and author from Winnipeg, Manitoba, Canada. She is a contributing writer for *Daily Guideposts,* and her latest book is *Peeking Through the Knothole: Scenes for the Soul from the 1940s.*

Debbie Bentley ("What My Students Taught Me") is a retired teacher and a freelance writer.

Judy Burford ("Never Good Enough") and her husband raise beef cattle in Louisiana. They have two daughters, one son-in-law, and two fabulous grandchildren. Judy enjoys teaching Sunday school, singing in the choir, arranging flowers, writing, reading, and traveling.

BARBARA CURTIS ("Freedom Found") is a prolific mother and writer, with twelve children, seven books, and hundreds of published articles and columns. She has received three Amy Writing Awards as well as the 2004 Congressional Angel in Adoption Award. Visit her at her blog, *www.mommylife.net*.

CYNTHIA L. D'AGOSTINO ("Dirty Laundry") is a mother of five and grandmother of two. She and her husband, Paul, are raising their children in Independence, Missouri. Cynthia enjoys her family, her friends, and all of their stories.

KIMBERLY DAVIDSON ("The F.A.T. Girl in the Mirror") is an inspirational speaker, teacher, writer, and the founder of Olive Branch Outreach, which ministers to help people with eating disorders to glorify Jesus Christ. She is a women's ministry leader and seminary student.

ELSI DODGE ("Safely in His Hands"), a child of God, is a single retired teacher and has completed the Christian Writers Guild's apprentice and journeyman courses. She lives in Boulder, Colorado, and travels with her dog and cat in a thirty-foot RV.

ANITA ESTES ("Pilgrimage Home") is an art teacher, freelance writer, and book-club leader. She is honored in *Who's Who of American Teachers for 2000 and 2005*. Her writing appears in several publications, and she is the author of *When God Speaks*.

Melissa Fields ("The God Who Knocks with Kindness") is originally a Southern girl from Walton, West Virginia, who has worked in magazine publishing and now lives in central Massachusetts with her husband and two young children. Melissa is writing children's books focusing on family values, morals, and building confidence in children.

Sue Foster ("The High That Lasts") is a published author of short stories and articles. She serves as a ministering elder at Capistrano Community Church. Sue and her husband, Steve, reside in Laguna Niguel, California. They are the parents of two grown daughters.

Jo Franz ("Convicted at a Concert") is a speaker for retreats, conferences, and banquets, incorporating songs, some of which are original, into her presentations. Her stories appear in books, magazines, and her memoir. Contact her at *jofranz@aol.com* or visit her online at *www.jofranz.com*.

George Elias Galieh ("An Instrument God Uses") was granted an honorary doctorate from Cambridge College (U.S.A.) for his many years in Christian radio. His first love is preaching the Word to live audiences, using the arts in evangelism.

Rita Stella Galieh ("Fighting the Good Fight") is a gospel singer, graphic artist, and author of historical novels. She also cohosts a weekly radio program broadcast throughout Australia. Each year, Rita and her husband, George, visit Thailand to minister in Buddhist prisons, hospitals, and schools. On one of their journeys Somchai Soonthornturasuk served as their interpreter.

EVANGELINE BEALS GARDNER ("On the Trail to Truth") is a full-time stay-at-home mom who is also a freelance writer, sings on the worship team at church, and teaches piano lessons from her home. She met Suha Gibson in church Bible study.

CHERYL GOCHNAUER ("A Different Destiny") is founder of Homebodies, an online and print ministry for at-home parents. Sign up for her free weekly e-mail newsletter by writing *homebodies@comcast.net*.

MARION E. GORMAN ("New Life") is a novice writer who has been published in *Mature Years, Seek,* various newsletters, and the local paper. She lives with her husband, Jim, in rural Pennsylvania and thoroughly enjoys their nineteen grandchildren.

MARY A. HAKE ("Return to My Father" and "Seeking Security") has been published in newspapers, periodicals, on the Internet, and in several books. She does freelance editing from her home in Central Oregon and has taught writing at conferences and to schoolchildren.

ALBERT HALEY ("The Collision") is a Yale graduate and the author of *Home Ground: Stories of Two Families and the Land* and the novel *Exotic.* He serves as writer-in-residence at Abilene Christian University in Abilene, Texas, where he lives with his wife, Joyce, and son, Coleman.

CLEMENT HANSON ("Those Who Believe") practices occupational medicine and rehabilitation with Health One in Denver, Colorado. His wife, Mary, is a children's book writer and student at Denver Seminary. They are active members of Montview Boulevard Presbyterian Church. You can contact them at *hanson139@comcast.net*.

SONJA HERBERT ("Finding Christ at the Carnival") has written a biographical novel about her mother hiding in a circus during the Holocaust. She is also the author of several award-winning published stories. She has almost completed a memoir about her childhood.

RENÉE W. HIXSON ("Finding My Own Faith") and her family live on a small college campus in beautiful British Columbia. In teaching, speaking, writing, or just "hanging around," her passion is to show how Christ is real in today's culture.

WILLIE KANTHENGA ("Righteousness for the Right Reasons") is a news editor in Malawi for Trans World Radio, with the ultimate vision of being a Christian researcher and publisher. He and his wife Dorcas have two toddler sons.

MARA KIM ("Belonging to the Lord") resides in Washington with her husband and son. She enjoys hiking, reading, and spending quality time with her family. She is a member of American Christian Fiction Writers and Christian Writers Guild.

ARDY KOLB ("Learning to Give Up") and Jerry have five grown children. They owned a Christian bookstore for thirteen years, then sold it. Currently Ardy writes, edits, and does layout for the regional Prison Fellowship newsletter, as well as various other volunteer projects and freelance writing and editing.

THOMAS LACY ("A Worthwhile Life") went from a barstool to the Bible. He was ordained in 1978, and in 1985 founded New Hope Counseling Service along with his wife, Pat. He is a former chaplain of the Hanover County jail in Virginia.

DIANA LEE ("Hopeless to Hopeful") lives in Florida with her husband of forty-two years. They have four children and eight grandchildren. Diana is active in her church and enjoys cooking, music, and hiking.

B. J. LEFFALL-McGIBBONEY ("The Voice of the Future") is a widow with two grown children and two wonderful grandchildren. She is a clinical social worker in Greensboro, North Carolina. At the prompting of the Holy Spirit, Brenda is currently working on a book of devotions.

JEANETTE GARDNER LITTLETON ("Back from the Wild Side") is a full-time freelance writer and editor living in Kansas City. She enjoys working with a writers' group (*www.HACWN.org*) where she met Rick Stock, and his wife, Rhonda. Besides raising their own kids, Rick and Rhonda work with children and married couples in crisis at their church in Lenexa, Kansas.

MARK LITTLETON ("A Night Up in Smoke") is the author of more than eighty-five books and thousands of articles, poems, and devotionals. He is a full-time freelancer who lives in Kansas City with his wife and three children. He enjoys speaking at churches, and has won awards through Toastmasters. You can reach him at *MLittleton@earthlink.net*.

LYNN LUDWICK ("No Longer Adrift") lives with her husband and their one-eyed cat in a small southern-Oregon town. She enjoys writing, quilting, baking, gardening, and being Nana to her six grandchildren.

BECKY LYLES ("Set Free") is the author of *It's a God Thing! Inspiring Stories of Life-Changing Friendships* and *On a Wing and a Prayer: Stories from Freedom Fellowship, a Prison Ministry*. Gary Carlson is now with the Lord, but his testimony, like his new life in Christ, continues to give hope to those still in bondage.

SUSAN A. J. LYTTEK ("How I Found True Love"), wife of Gary since 1983, homeschooling mother of two boys, Erik and Karl, and coach for Write At Home, an Internet writing class for homeschoolers, snatches moments to write before the school day begins.

JOYCE STARR MACIAS ("The School Board Meeting That Changed My Life") divides her time between freelance writing and conducting nursing-home services. She is a retired newspaper reporter and is writing her second Christian novel. She graduated from college with high honors in 2000, at the age of sixty-seven.

MAXINE MARSOLINI ("When God Enters the Stepfamily") is the author of *Raising Children in Blended Families* (Kregel Publications 2006), *Blended Families* (Moody Press 2000), and the *Blended Families Workbook* (Pleasant Word 2004). Most stepfamilies need help to live in harmony. As an author and speaker, Maxine brings enthusiasm, experience, and positive help to stepfamilies issues. Visit *www.blendedfamilies.net*.

SHANA L. MERRISS ("He Knew Me") lives in Murray, Kentucky, with her husband of ten years and their three sons. She works part time at a church preschool/mother's day out program and enjoys reading and spending time with friends.

PAM MEYERS ("Like Son, Like Father") has published articles in *Today's Christian Woman* and *Ancestry* magazines and serves on the board of the American Christian Fiction Writers. Recently retired, Pam now devotes more time to writing and is working on her third novel. She also serves as an interpreter for the deaf at her church, where Frank and Barb Coppaletta also attend.

KURT A. MIESNER ("Change of Heart") is a 1994 graduate of the United States Military Academy at West Point. After enjoying a successful career in the 1st Cavalry Division, Kurt separated from the army as a captain in 1999. He got his master's degree from Pittsburg State University, and now he and his wife Davi live in Fort Smith, Arkansas.

ELIZABETH MONTES ("God and the Marriage Mess") lives in Washington State with her loving husband, Marlo. They have two grown children and one kindergartener. Marlo continues to serve in the United States Army.

HAROLD E. MORGAN ("The Measure of a Man"), a graduate of Oklahoma Baptist University, established and pastored churches in Oklahoma, Kansas, and Missouri for thirty-two years. He has had devotionals and articles published in *Preacher's Magazine*, *The Secret Place*, and *Advance*. A novel, *Victims of Hate*, is still in process. He and his wife have four children, twelve grandchildren, and eleven great-grandchildren.

JAN POTTER ("Forever Safe") is a homemaker/freelance writer in Phoenix, Arizona. Her articles have appeared in many publications, including *Discipleship Journal, Moody*, and *Today's Christian Woman*. She also co-leads a military ministry at her church—praying for troops, sending letters, and mailing packages to those overseas.

SUSAN J. REINHARDT ("Clean at Last: Inside and Out") and her husband reside in the northeastern United States. Her work has appeared in *The RevWriter Resource* and *Honey From the Rock* tape ministry. She enjoys reading and antiquing.

CAROLINE SEUNGHEE ROBERTS ("When Excelling Isn't Enough") lives with her husband Bob, her daughter Elena and sons Ian, Evan, Elijah, Jonathan, and Joshua in East Tennessee.

DAVID R. SIMERSON ("The Silent Sentinel") has applied his spiritual gifts as a lay author, speaker, and workshop facilitator for the past fifteen years, while developing men's ministries and evangelism training programs. He is a Gideon and a Promise Keeper.

EVELYN RHODES SMITH ("Daddy's Girl") resides in Charleston, West Virginia, with her husband, Ted, a chemical engineer. Evelyn and Ted are both active at the Bible Center Church, teaching and encoding services for the Internet.

GAY SORENSEN ("Born Again? Oh No!") belongs to Calvary Chapel in Olympia, Washington, where she writes a monthly column for the church newsletter. She has three children, five grandchildren, four great-grandchildren, and one cat, all of whom inspire her writings.

MICHELE STARKEY ("From the Good Life to a Better Life") suffered a ruptured brain aneurysm but survived by the grace of God. She and her beloved husband, Keith, live in the Hudson Valley of New York, where they enjoy life to the fullest.

LYNN M. STOUT ("Losing Control to Find It") lives in the East Tennessee mountains with her husband of sixteen years, two precious daughters, and entirely too many pets. Her nonfiction appears in several small Christian publications. Visit her blog at *http://isa268.blogspot.com.*

KAREN STRAND ("Faith in My Sleeve") has published articles and poems in a wide variety of publications, including *Moody Magazine*, *Decision*, and *Focus on the Family*. Learn more at her Web site, *www.karenstrand.com.* Karen has corresponded with Pastor Prem Chand Daniel for the past twenty years. She has a special place in her heart for Jammu and Kashmir, India, the least-evangelized region of that country.

RONICA STROMBERG ("Missing Person—Found by God" and "Drawn by Love") is the author of the children's book *The Glass Inheritance* and has written stories appearing in ten anthologies. She met Michelle Steele while working at a local newspaper.